TRADE
AND TRADE POLICY
FOR
DEVELOPMENT

PRAEGER SERIES
ON
INTERNATIONAL ECONOMICS
AND
DEVELOPMENT

ISAIAH FRANK
CONSULTING EDITOR

TRADE
AND TRADE POLICY
FOR
DEVELOPMENT

STAFFAN BURENSTAM LINDER

FREDERICK A. PRAEGER, *Publishers*
New York • Washington • London

Frederick A. Praeger, Publishers

111 Fourth Avenue, New York, N.Y. 10003, U.S.A.
77–79 Charlotte Street, London W. 1, England

Published in the United States of America in 1967
by Frederick A. Praeger, Inc., Publishers

© 1967 by Frederick A. Praeger, Inc.

This book was first published in a Spanish-language
edition by the Centro de Estudios Monetarios Latinoamericanos, Mexico City.

Library of Congress Catalog Card Number: 66–26552

Printed in the United States of America

To
Charles P. Kindleberger

Contents

Preface

The effects of international trade on underdeveloped countries pose many problems of both practice and theory. Despite much discussion, however, there is little agreement on what in fact an adequate trade theory for underdeveloped areas would be. Strongly formulated opposing views have been advanced, and, in this situation, some of the texts on development economics conveniently bypass the issue by employing vague generalities.

There are many reasons for this state of affairs. To begin with, there exists a neatly woven trade theory—the neoclassical trade theory, with a number of modifications to allow the incorporation of Keynesian theory. Although originally formulated to explain the effects of trade on countries that happened to be industrially advanced, this theory exerts a powerful influence on attempts to theorize about the trade of other types of countries. Although it is not self-evident that the neoclassical theory is inadequate for this purpose, many economists have considered it inapplicable to the conditions of underdeveloped countries and have put forward a variety of alternative theories—alternative not only to neoclassical theory but also to one another. The ensuing confusion is increased for two additional reasons. First, even if neoclassical theory can be criticized, it is nonetheless obvious that *elements of it* are of the greatest significance for underdeveloped countries; the rejection of neoclassical theory thus cannot be carried out indiscriminately. Second, underdeveloped nations do not constitute a homogeneous group the conditions of which can be handled easily in a single theory.

The present study represents, hopefully, a link in the chain of attempts to provide a more secure theoretical basis for thinking about trade and underdeveloped countries. First, as a compromise between generality and applicability, recognizing the wide differences among underdeveloped countries, two different models of trade have been formulated: the one will cover "developing" countries or regions; the other, "backward" countries or regions. Second, it has been found necessary to pay great attention to conventional trade theory, too, in order simultaneously to show exactly why this theory cannot be accepted as a general theory and to determine which parts must be incorporated into any other approach.

To some extent, work on this study represents the development of some ideas embodied in an earlier book, *An Essay on Trade and Transformation*.[1] For instance, I make use of the theory of "representative demand" to explain why the relative price structures of developing and advanced countries may show certain characteristics that might mean that the export possibilities for developing countries are much more limited than is usually concluded on the basis of the comparative-cost theory—a theory that is misleading in its total disregard of *absolute* productivities. The trade theory for backward countries also represents the direct use of ideas formulated in the earlier book.

Active writing on this monograph has occupied me for three years, three very pleasant years, in fact.* My first period of research heightened the attractiveness to me of a most interesting year as visiting associate professor at Columbia University in 1962–63. The first tentative hypotheses I developed during that period formed the basis for papers read at seminars at Harvard University, the Massachusetts Institute of Technology, the University of Michigan, and Wesleyan University. I was then invited to Mexico City to give a series of seminars at the Centro de Estudios Monetarios Latinoamericanos (CEMLA). During a three-month period in the summer of 1963, I worked for the U. N. at Geneva to prepare a paper

---

*This applies as far as I can understand, to my family, too—a remarkable fact, if I am to judge from most prefaces to scholarly works.

on the significance of the General Agreement on Tariffs and Trade (GATT) for underdeveloped countries as part of the documentation for the Conference on Trade and Development. This research proved helpful to me in working on this manuscript. During the later stage of writing, I read papers in Stockholm, Helsinki, and Uppsala. In the summer of 1965, I again lectured in Mexico (at El Colegio de Mexico) and in Japan on the problems explored in this study. I wish to record not only the pleasure and stimulus I received from these various adventures, but also my gratitude to all those who helped me on those occasions through their constructive criticism.

I have also accumulated a great debt to those who assisted me in other ways during my active work on this book. I wish, in particular, to express my thanks to Mr. Paul Huber, presently of the National Planning Association in Washington, D. C., who made many useful criticisms of the manuscript and suggested a number of corrections and improvements; to Mr. David Lones, who took the trouble of correcting my English; to Mrs. Kerstin Johanson, who checked all quotations and references, assembled the bibliography, and assisted in a number of other ways; to Mr. Bengt Berg, who drew the figures and diagrams; and to Miss Brita Modin, who carefully typed what to both of us seemed to be a never-ending flow of versions of this manuscript.

While working on this study, I received a scholarship from the Swedish Institute for Bank Research and a grant from the Swedish Social Science Research Council. In various ways, generous support has also been provided by the Stockholms Enskilda Bank. For all this, which greatly facilitated undisturbed concentration on the task at hand, I am most grateful.

Finally, this book has been dedicated to Charles P. Kindleberger—inspirer and innovator and, I respectfully hope, my friend.

STAFFAN BURENSTAM LINDER

Stockholm
June, 1966

I

Introduction

The actual commercial policies followed by underdeveloped countries show little resemblance to the suggested commercial policies that can be derived from the
hard core of international-trade theory as set out in the
standard works.[1] "Free trade in principle," which would
be the prescription of the conventional theory (i.e., the
neoclassical theory with Keynesian amendments), is not
applied.

The possible explanation of the fact that commercial
policies of underdeveloped countries are characterized
by a multitude of tariffs, quotas, and exchange restrictions rather than by free trade could be any of the following three:

1. The conventional theory offers a reasonable approximation of the role of trade, but actual policies are badly
designed, being the result of short-run political expediency rather than rational economic thinking.

2. Modifications of the free-trade principle, recognized in more sophisticated versions of the conventional
theory itself, could be considered so important in the application of the theory to underdeveloped countries as to
make exceptions become the rule. Optimum policy, although based on the conventional theory, will then look
very different from the commercial-policy principle usually associated with that theory. Whether or not the policies actually pursued in underdeveloped countries can be
regarded as optimum ones in the light of the theoretical
modifications of the free-trade principle is, of course,
another question. However, according to this explanation, the fact that the actual policies are characterized
by restrictions rather than by free trade does not *necessarily* mean that they are suboptimal.

3. The conventional commercial-policy doctrine might be inapplicable for reasons not recognized within its own theoretical framework.

In discussing the role of trade in development processes and the commercial policies of underdeveloped countries, one can find examples of arguments along each of these three lines. For instance, Haberler and Viner have strongly argued, on the basis of conventional theory, that present policies of underdeveloped countries in the trade field are misguided.[2] Hagen's modernization of the Manoilesco argument for protection (which was later used by Baldwin, among others) represents a typical case in which the modifications of the free-trade rule are extended so far as to change completely the basic, outward characteristics of the suggested conventional commercial policy.[3] Infant-industry tariffs and optimum tariffs to improve the terms of trade constitute other well-recognized, and for underdeveloped countries possibly quite relevant, exceptions to the free-trade principle. Finally, a number of writers have rejected the standard theory and produced a variety of alternative theoretical explanations of the effects of international trade on underdeveloped countries.[4] Thus, there is sharp disagreement on basic issues in trade policy. It is symptomatic that the treatment of the role of trade in the literature on economic development is typically vague.

The position taken in this study falls within the third category—i.e., that conventional trade theory is not a suitable tool for analyzing the effects of trade on underdeveloped countries and for formulating their commercial policies. An alternative approach will be developed.

Conventional theory is inadequate because its analytical apparatus is geared solely to the question of the welfare and structural effects of the reallocation of given, fully utilized resources resulting from changes in relative prices in connection with trade. This delimitation of the problem area assumes a full utilization of the economic potential in the nation concerned—an assumption that can be made on the basis of the main conclusion in

balance-of-payments theory: namely, that through optimum expenditure policies (i.e., a certain mix of economic
policies affecting prices and incomes), internal and external equilibrium can be simultaneously maintained. To
the extent this conclusion can be upheld, it is natural to
look on trade and trade policy as a means of optimizing
the allocation of resources, giving no more attention to
their effects on growth than what follows from the assumption that static efficiency in allocation is a precondition for dynamic efficiency in growth.[5]

With respect to the effects of trade on underdeveloped
countries, this approach must be reconsidered. The
crucial question is whether the economic potential can be
fully utilized at the same time that external equilibrium
is maintained. There are two reasons why this may not,
in fact, be the case. First, reallocation of factors of
production may not be possible because of extreme fric-
tions, and if the factors of production are employed at
subsistence incomes, it may be impossible to maintain
production in a sector that has experienced an unfavorable shift in relative prices. Second, certain imports may
be required in certain proportions to achieve the full
utilization of the economic potential, and these imports
may exceed exports. In both these cases, the effects of
trade not only on the utilization of existing factors, but
also on factor growth, will differ greatly from what they
are supposed to be according to conventional theory.
Trade and trade policy cannot be attributed the role of
optimization of allocation.

Both these mechanisms preventing the simultaneous
maintenance of internal and external equilibrium probably affect all underdeveloped countries to some extent.
But it is likely that the first mechanism—inability to reallocate productive factors at subsistence incomes—is
most noticeable. For only when an underdeveloped nation
reaches the stage where there is determination and rea-
lism in its development effort does the requirement of
imports to operate and expand the production apparatus
arise; and not until then does the second mechanism

—import requirements exceeding export earnings—become important. (At the same time, the capacity to reallocate increases, incomes rise above the subsistence level, and the first mechanism therefore decreases in importance.)

A nation's degree of development or underdevelopment is thus of major importance with respect to the effect of trade on its economy. Although it is possible to construct one general model for trade in underdeveloped countries, combining the widely different effects of the two mechanisms, it might be convenient, in order to gain in simplicity, to formulate *two models* applicable to different kinds of underdeveloped countries. In this way, the extreme differences among underdeveloped countries, to the consequences of which lip service but not practical attention in theoretical work is usually paid, would be underlined.

The two kinds of countries would be referred to as "backward countries" and "developing countries." Although it could be expected that a backward country will eventually become a "developing" one, and although this should be hoped for, it will not necessarily occur in fact. This means that the two models should not be considered as necessarily representing an organic sequence.

It must be understood that this dual classification does not represent an attempt to bifurcate all underdeveloped countries into two neat and easily recognizable groups. Instead, backward and developing countries must be regarded as representing two typical, extreme forms on the scale. Between these two poles, there is a variety of intermediate cases. Furthermore, it should be understood that this differentiation *ought not to be made so much in terms of countries as in terms of regions or sectors.* An underdeveloped country usually consists of a backward and a developing part; the relative size of these two parts determines whether the country should be labeled as backward or developing; a developing country is, thus, a country with an important developing region or sector in its economy. For the sake of simplicity, however, reference will be made only to developing or backward countries. Examples of nations with important developing sectors are Mexico, Brazil, and India, although the economy of each of these includes a substantial backward sector. It should also be recognized that these sectors will be affected by trade in different ways.

The main emphasis in this study will be on the second category of countries, and for a variety of reasons. Although there are probably fewer of these, they are the most populous and, from a political standpoint, the most important in the "underdeveloped regions." Second, the future of underdeveloped countries hinges on the fortunes of developing regions or sectors. Third, the analysis of the role of trade in developing countries is of greater theoretical interest because it requires a more definite break with conventional theory, while at the same time retaining orthodox analysis in other aspects. Furthermore, the commercial-policy problems of these countries are, compared with those of backward countries, both more complicated and of greater significance. It will be shown that trade in the former has a potentially important leverage effect on capacity utilization. The role of trade will emerge as one of a *potential superengine*. And, last, the author has already discussed elsewhere the implications for trade theory of a combined assumption of subsistence incomes and no reallocative ability, the chief characteristic of backward countries.[6] In that study, however, the objective was, not to derive commercial-policy conclusions, but simply to demonstrate theoretically that, contrary to established orthodoxy,[7] the main conclusions of the neoclassical reallocation theory could not easily be upheld in cases where there was no ability to reallocate production factors employed at subsistence incomes.

As already pointed out, there is nothing startling in the assertion that conventional trade theory is inapplicable to underdeveloped countries. Since many economists have written in this vein, especially economists from the underdeveloped countries themselves, there can be no pretention that what is to be said in this study is wholly novel. On the contrary, as will be seen, the conclusions to be derived from the two models are related to the more or less unorthodox views on trade and underdeveloped countries, such as those presented by H. Kitamura, I. G. Patel, S. J. Patel, and V. L. Urquidi—forming a rather distinct group; and R. Prebisch, H. Myint, R. Nurkse, and D. Seers—representing a much more heterogeneous group.[8] But, if there are such similarities, what, then, are the ambitions of this study?

First, the intention is to bring greater order into this often quite confusing discussion, where there is a conflict not only between conventional theory and alternative trade theories but also, or so it seems, between various unconventional theories. Within an analytical framework built on the distinction between developing and backward countries, it can be shown that the various unorthodox theories are not mutually exclusive, but they do, in fact, cover different cases.

Second, the various existing unconventional theories can be improved on. They can be made more rigorous—by defining the exact conditions under which the trade theory to be subsequently formulated is applicable, and by stating precisely why conventional theory is not a good approximation under these circumstances. This intention presupposes some theoretical innnovations. For instance, to substantiate the theory suggested for developing countries, certain modifications must be introduced into the comparative-cost doctrine *even within its own static framework.*

Evidence that such an improvement is necessary lies in the fact that these unorthodox theories, suggested primarily by economists in underdeveloped countries, have never exerted any strong influence on the hard core of trade theory as taught in universities in economically advanced countries, despite the fact that the views of these economists should carry a great deal of weight, formed as they are with firsthand empirical knowledge.

But they have failed to affect the main stream of trade theory since, to be efficient and intellectually convincing, an implicit or explicit attack on conventional theory must be based on theorizing of a more systematic kind. Theories on trade in underdeveloped countries will never be regarded as anything but assertions, so long as it is not carefully explained why existing theory cannot be used as a general theory applied with equal validity to developed and less developed countries. For instance, the claim, so often made, that underdeveloped countries need trade restrictions for balance-of-payments reasons can be, and is, as a matter of routine, refuted within the framework of conventional trade theory. To advocate such trade restrictions, one must carefully rebut the conventional refutation, not just deny it.

Third, and this is a special aspect of the formulation of more rigorous theory, it is necessary to define exactly under what circumstances and to what extent conventional theory is, in fact, applicable to underdeveloped countries. For conventional theory should not be rejected flatly; acid assertions of the total nonapplicability of conventional theory result in serious mistakes and in "throwing out the baby with the bath water." For instance, it is obvious that even if the conventional balance-of-payments theory must be rejected because simultaneous internal and external equilibrium cannot be guaranteed, it nonetheless offers important insights. Another instance is the interesting use that can be made of conventional trade theory in formulating a customs-union theory for developing countries (although, in view of the special conditions of such nations, it will show paradoxical differences from conventional customs-union theory).

Finally, a more systematic trade theory would provide a basis for formulating more systematic policies. It could also influence the trade and aid policies pursued by economically advanced countries. So long as an alternative trade theory has not been worked out more rigorously, it cannot be expected that policies

which are important for underdeveloped countries will
be informed by a thorough understanding of those countries' foreign-trade situation.

II

A Theory of Trade for
Developing Countries

The category of developing countries as we shall
define them here is made up of countries that, although
they have all the usual characteristics of *under*developed countries, also have a reasonable chance of a self-
sustained growth process which will eventually turn
them into advanced economies. "Developing" is thus
not a euphemism.

The characteristic effect of trade on such countries
will be assumed to be that, fully to utilize their existing
resources and their growth potential, they require certain
imports that it may prove impossible to acquire through
exports of equal value. The simultaneous establishment
of internal and external equilibrium is thus not possible.

In this reformulation, it is necessary to distinguish
between (1) trade with advanced countries and (2) trade
with other underdeveloped countries. On this basis,
most attention will be paid in this chapter to the effects
of trade with advanced countries, not because this kind
of trade is necessarily the most important, but because
the role of this trade differs most, in practice, from the
role given it in conventional theory. Furthermore, the
conclusions to be drawn from the analysis of trade with
advanced countries bear upon any assessment of trade
with other underdeveloped countries; in fact, it is this
particular influence that creates interesting differences
between conventional theory and a theory of trade for
developing countries. But it is convenient—mainly for
critical purposes, but also for positive use—to sum-
marize the main characteristics of the conventional
theory referred to throughout this study.

In this study, "conventional trade theory" is understood to mean the neoclassical reallocation theory with

Keynesian amendments. The balance-of-payments part of this theory explains how changes particularly in price and income levels, absolutely and in relation to other countries, affect the balance of payments. Special attention is devoted to how such changes can be induced through economic-policy measures (exchange-rate variations, etc.) designed to manipulate the balance of payments or, more specifically, to establish external equilibrium concurrently with internal equilibrium.

On the basis of the finding that external equilibrium and internal equilibrium can be simultaneously established, the conventional analysis of the welfare and structural effects of international trade is limited to the effects of the reallocation of fully employed resources. According to it, the opening up of trade will expose a country to a different set of relative commodity prices, which will affect both production and consumption patterns.

On the production side, there will be a reallocation of existing factors of production so that more relatively inexpensive goods will be produced, and fewer expensive ones. In more technical terms, the reallocation moves the economy along a production-possibility function away from the former production point, where the marginal rate of transformation in production equaled the marginal rate of substitution in consumption, to one where it equals the marginal rate of transformation through trade.

On the consumption side, there will be a corresponding change. Technically speaking, there will be a movement away from the former consumption point, where the marginal rate of substitution in consumption equaled the marginal rate of transformation in production, to one where it equals the marginal rate of transformation through trade.

These production and consumption changes have certain welfare effects, which will be examined more carefully in a later chapter. Suffice it to say here that it can be shown that welfare can be increased through trade and the reallocation of resources. This increase is important for a study of the structural effects, since, in addition to the relative price changes, it will influence consumption and, thus, production, too.

This theory is so well known and has been summarized so often that it is unnecessary to go beyond this statement of its basic elements. But it is important to note that it deals essentially with the effects of marginal changes in the use of existing, fully utilized resources. Growth effects are introduced only to the extent that the implications of the optimization of allocation (static efficiency) for increasing factor totals (dynamic efficiency) have been taken into account.[1]

TRADE WITH ADVANCED COUNTRIES

The Import Minimum: A Factor-Proportions Problem

When a backward country becomes a developing country, the possibility for the rational use of significant quantities of capital goods emerges. The need for capital goods can be filled to only a minor extent by domestic production. And the obstacles to the transformation of domestic factors of production into capital goods are characteristic features of countries not yet economically advanced. The development process then requires certain *expansion imports*, in the absence of which the growth potential (in the form of a net savings potential) could not be fully exploited, and, in order to keep existing capacity unchanged and to avoid the frustration of savings for reinvestment, *reinvestment imports*, in the form of capital goods to replace former expansion imports; together, these constitute *investment imports*. In order fully to utilize existing capacity, there must also be certain *operation imports*—spare parts to imported capital goods and nondomestic primary products. Reinvestment and operation imports together constitute *maintenance im-*

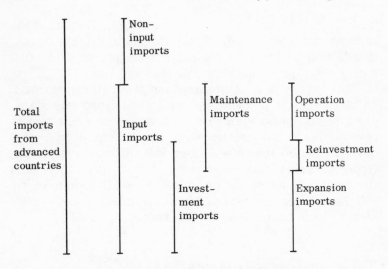

ports. All these *input imports* are assumed to be necessary to avoid underutilization of existing resources and
frustration of the growth potential, and it is assumed
they can be secured only from advanced countries.

It is obvious that, in actual practice, it may be difficult to determine which imports are input imports. It
would be necessary to evaluate the domestic production
possibilities and the final use of the various import
items. But for all practical purposes, it can be simply
argued that imported capital goods and industrial raw
materials constitute input imports. Certain exceptions
to this rule can be specified. Consumer goods that cannot
be produced in sufficient quantities domestically and
are basic necessities, required to maintain the labor
force in the developing country or sector, qualify as input imports, or, more precisely, as operation imports.
On the other hand, *all* capital goods are not input imports,
since some such goods can be produced domestically.[2]
Furthermore, it may be possible for some raw materials
to be produced domestically, at least to some extent,
even though they are being imported. (The subsequent
discussion will clarify the meaning of the requirement
that, in order to qualify as an input import, a good must

not be producible domestically.) In principle, goods are not producible if the domestic factors involved do not obtain minimum rewards to subsist. The extreme case occurs when a negative value is added—when imports required for production represent a higher foreign-exchange cost than the importation of the end products in question.

It is also difficult to classify input imports in various subcategories. For instance, it is not self-evident whether imports to a domestic capital-goods industry should be classified as operation imports or investment imports. Imports for inventory purposes could also be classified in different ways. But the distinctions between the different input categories are at least as clear, conceptually as well as practically, as many other distinctions in current use—between savings and consumption, for instance.

The input-import requirement constitutes a *factor-proportions problem*, which, if not solved, would lead to underemployment of existing resources and frustrate the accumulation of further resources. A factor-proportions problem arises when factor substitutability is not great enough to allow purposeful employment of all existing or potentially existing factors of production. (By "potentially existing" factors I mean factors that would have been brought into existence had there been no factor-proportions problem.) Eckaus, who first focused attention on a factor-proportions problem in the context of development economics,[3] was concerned with explaining underemployment that is not due to lack of effective demand and that exists along with the widespread use of capital-intensive techniques. Such a situation could arise, and be given a rational explanation, he argued, if there were limited factor substitutability and the capital/labor proportions were such that all labor could not be employed.

The factor-proportions problem to which attention is being brought here is, however, of a different nature. It arises out of limited substitutability, not between capital and labor, but between domestic factors and the input imports. The domestic factors that may be unemployed if there is a lack of input imports are not only labor but also *capital resources* (including capital goods that have been imported in earlier periods). As to labor, only the quantity that can be purposefully employed together with available capital resources will be counted among domestic factors. This amount is a function of the amount of capital resources and the substitutability between capital and labor. The factor-proportions problem that is emphasized here thus does not preclude a parallel Eckaus factor-proportions problem, too.

At this stage, it might be useful not merely to assume that there are nonreplaceable input imports but to ask *why* there seems to be such a limited substitutability between domestic factors and input imports, i.e., why there should be an input-import requirement at all. To begin with, it is obvious that if there are primary commodities that cannot be produced domestically, they qualify as input imports and must be obtained in a certain, probably inflexible, proportion to existing domestic factors. As to capital goods, the need to import for maintenance purposes is a derived need: i.e., if capital goods must be imported for expansion purposes, there must also be imports for maintenance purposes. The important question, thus, is why there must be expansion imports at all. In fact, it is not at all obvious why a developing country should need, for expansion, a certain proportion of modern equipment that it cannot produce. Yet it is noticeable that developing countries wish to use the most modern techniques in their investment programs rather than simple techniques that could be introduced with domestically produced capital equipment. The reasons for this preference (similar to the preference for capital-intensive techniques over labor-intensive ones) is more or less rational. It is no doubt easy to find examples of considerations of prestige entering into the choice of technology. There is a "demonstration effect" influencing the demand for capital goods perhaps even more strongly than the demand for consumer goods.

However, when considering the alternative of simple techniques, it must be recognized that they cannot simply be taken over from presently advanced countries. The technology from the initial periods of these countries' industrialization is now not only economically antiquated but effectively forgotten. Simple techniques would, thus, in a great majority of cases, require a substantial amount of inventive and engineering work in the developing countries themselves. Even if this could be done, using available domestic factors, it would be so time-consuming that it would probably not impress policy-makers as politically feasible, even if methods of using capital goods that do not require advanced technology and could be produced at home were, *in the end*, to prove more effective.

Thus, the low level of development makes it both impossible for the country to produce advanced capital equipment and, in order to advance as fast as is deemed necessary, imperative for it to use such equipment. Whether attitudes of this kind should be referred to as "rational" is irrelevant for the specific purposes of this study. The intention here is to discuss the role of trade in countries where, for whatever the reasons, the substitutability between domestic factors and certain imported inputs is, or is treated as, limited.

Clearly, the lack of substitutability between the two factors of production need not be complete. Even if there were a fixed proportion of input imports and domestic factors in each industry, it is most unlikely that this proportion would be the same in all industries. Variations in the production mix would then give some flexibility, but, to the extent that growth must be balanced between the different industries and sectors of the economy—whether balanced at each moment, as in the balanced-growth doctrine, or at intervals, à la Hirschman—the possibilities of securing a certain substitutability by varying the production mix will be few.[4] And, even if there were such possibilities and even if there were opportunities for varying the proportion of input imports *within* the different industries, a country might still, of course, face a factor-proportions problem. This situation would arise when the substitution of domestic factors for imported inputs could not be carried any further. There would then be some minimum proportion of imported inputs that must be secured to utilize domestic factors and develop the growth potential.

The implications of the factor-proportions problem on capacity use and growth can be expressed more precisely in algebraic terms. The level of operation inputs required to maintain full capacity use can be expressed as $M_0^+ = p\bar{C}$. Here, M_0^+ is the required minimum of operation imports; $\bar{C}$, total capacity, or rather the potential maximum flow of services from existing capacity; and p the fraction of operation imports required per unit of domestic factors ($p = M_0/C$). To the extent $M_0 < M_0^+$, where M_0 is equal to the actual amount of operation imports, there will be a lack of operation imports, which will act as a limitation on capacity use. Actual capacity use will be $C = M_0/p$. If both sides are divided by $\bar{C}$, an expression for the percentage use of full capacity is obtained. We thus have an expression for capacity utilization as determined by imports for operation purposes.

The maximum flow of services from existing capacity ($\bar{C}$) depends not only on the stock of domestic factors but also on the desired intensity in the utilization of these factors, e.g., the number of shifts per day that the existing capital goods are assumed to be worked. If the desired intensity is three shifts per day rather than one, the potential flow will be higher, and proportionally more operation imports will be needed. In contrasting the Eckaus capital/labor-proportions problem with that examined here, it can be pointed out that the Eckaus problem can be solved, or alleviated, through the greater use of existing capital equipment. Employment of this method would, however, mean that the need for input imports would increase; thus, it does not represent any solution to an input-import factor-proportions problem.

As to the utilization of the growth potential, it can be

assumed that capacity growth is determined by a number of factors, one of which is the *ex-ante* propensity to save out of a full-capacity income. This particular factor is interesting in the present context, as the translation of these savings into investments requires (1) a minimum amount of operation imports to reach full-capacity income, and (2) certain investment imports. The need for investment imports represents a net addition to the requirement of input imports, assuming that the need for operation imports is unaffected by the extent to which domestic capacity is being operated for consumption or investment purposes.

Assuming that there are no capital imports ($I_f = 0$), the minimum amount of *investment* imports required to avoid a frustration of *ex-ante* savings is $M_i^+ = m \, s_p \, \overline{Y} = m I_d^+$. Here, M_i^+ is required investment imports; s_p, the *ex-ante* propensity to save (gross); $\overline{Y}$ full-capacity income; m, the fraction of investment imports required per unit of domestic investment ($m = M_i/I_d$); and I_d^+, the required level of gross domestic investment to match *ex-ante* savings. It should be noted that if domestic factors can be used for investment purposes, m will be smaller than one and that, in this case, M_i^+ will be smaller than I_d^+.

If $M_i < M_i^+$, where M_i is equal to the actual amount of investment imports, there will be a lack of investment imports, which will act as a limitation on capacity growth. It will also mean that, to the extent that resources in a domestic capital-goods sector cannot be reallocated into the consumption-goods sector, there may be some non-usable output from this domestic capital-goods sector. The following equation specifies actual savings and investments:

$$sY = I_d = M_i/m,$$

where s is the *ex-post* propensity to save (gross).

If M_i is smaller than not only M_i^+ but also M_r^+ (i.e., the required *r*einvestment imports), there will be a decline in capacity, net investments being negative. The net change in capacity can be specified as $s'Y = I'd = (M_i - M_r^+)/m$, where the primes indicate net values. Divided by the total capital stock, the expression is changed into a specification of the actual *rate* of change in capacity. If $M_i < M_r^+$, there will, of course, also be a negative rate of change in capacity.

However, even if the required amount of investment imports could actually be secured, the actual rate of growth need not be high enough to qualify as "socially acceptable." Whether this rate of growth is at, or above, the socially acceptable minimum rate of growth will depend upon whether the additions of domestic factors in each period are sufficient. If, for instance, the *ex-ante* propensity to save is low, the actual rate of growth will, at least in the absence of capital imports, be low (and the required amount of input imports will be low). The maximum rate of growth will thus mirror the variety of elements other than international trade that determine what can be achieved in the economy. It can thus be seen how this model, which concentrates on the effects of international trade, can be fitted into a wider analytical framework designed to handle simultaneously a larger number of factors shaping the development.

If there are, in fact, certain capital imports, i.e., if the foreign investments of the developing country (I_f) are negative, there have to be certain modifications in the above expressions, because total savings (S) are no longer equal to, but are smaller than, I_d. If it is assumed that $s_p Y$ is unchanged, it is evident that I_d^+ must increase and will be equal to $s_p Y - I_f$ (which, because I_f is negative, represents a higher amount of domestic investment). To effectuate this increase in required investments, there must be an increase in required input imports. However, this increase will be smaller than the increase in required investments and will only amount to mI_f, the balance being covered by otherwise frustrated additions to domestic factors. The fact that capital imports increase the need for input imports by less than the amount of the capital imports themselves means that there can be an increase in actual input imports in relation to required input imports, the one being possible to increase by I_f, the other only increasing by mI_f. Thus, up to the point where all potential increases in domestic factors are being realized, capital imports have a leverage effect on capacity growth. There is, however, one important reservation to the whole of this argument, namely, that capital imports will create a new kind of input imports, i.e., remittances for servicing purposes. The effects of capital imports, notably the net effect on the rate of growth, will be explored in detail in later sections.[5]

The frustration of savings that will occur if $M_i < M_i^+$ is an important phenomenon. The frustration would manifest itself in a reduction of savings below their $s_p Y$ level, either through a fall in aggregate income (a decrease in expenditure below the full-capacity level), as would occur if the country had faced a Keynesian problem of insufficient effective demand, or through a decrease in the propensity to save (a redirection of expenditure).[6] If it is assumed that there is a fall in aggregate income (for instance, by discontinuing production of that part of the domestic capital-goods output that cannot be used, for lack of complementary investment imports), actual savings will be reduced with a constant propensity to save. It should be noted that the reduction in income implies a reduction in operation imports below their required level, and that this fall could lead to an increase in investment imports.[7] At some stage, there will be an equilibrium between actual savings and investment imports.

There is one peculiar feature of this particular process of adjustment through income reductions—namely, that there will be some investments taking place even though existing capacity is not being fully used. Although there may be situations where this might be rational as a matter of economic policy, we should assume that economic policy is geared rather to the task of assuring full utilization of existing capacity before investments take place. For the country is in a situation where, contrary to

Keynesian doctrine, an increase in investments does not
stimulate full capacity use, but takes place *at the expense
of* capacity use. This means that the reduction in savings
would instead come through a decline in the propensity
to save. An adjustment of this kind can occur not only to
the extent the propensity to save falls concurrently with
a reduction in aggregate income but also, and more interestingly, to the extent that savers and investors are
the same individuals or institutions—i.e., entrepreneurs
saving out of profits or public institutions saving out of
tax revenues. In this case, the lack of investment imports
might mean that planned savings will not be attempted.[8]
When faced with investment difficulties, entrepreneurs,
including the public sector, might change their expenditure plans and increase consumption. Under these circumstances, which are likely to prevail in developing
countries, with their underdeveloped credit market and
important public sector, the propensity to save is a function of the availability of investment imports, and aggregate income does not fall when planned savings exceed
ex-post savings, provided that at least the need for operation imports can be covered.

It should be noted that, in traditional theory, a lack of
domestic investment opportunities in relation to *ex-ante*
savings is said to create tendencies toward an export
surplus, i.e., toward foreign investment. In the framework
used here, however, this is not the case, because in the
first place, savings are frustrated owing to the M_i/m constraint (i.e., to a lack of import opportunities), which is,
of course, incompatible with an export surplus.

The total need for input imports can now be expressed
as $M_I^+ = M_0^+ + M_i^+ = p\overline{C} + ms_p\,\overline{Y}$. Since $\overline{Y}$ can be substituted
for $\overline{C}$, the expression can be rewritten $M_I^+ = \overline{Y}(p + ms_p)$.[9]
This required minimum of input imports changes, how-
ever, through time. To begin with, changes in $\overline{Y}$ will affect the import minimum. If $\overline{Y}$ decreases, a smaller
amount of input imports will be needed to operate and
maintain the size of the production apparatus. In the next
period, there will be a smaller income out of which to

generate potential additions to domestic factors, which would require expansion imports if they are not to be frustrated. A smaller amount of expansion imports will thus be needed. For the opposite reasons, the input-import requirements increase if $\overline{Y}$ increases through time.

However, if, in order to eliminate this particular effect, the input-import requirement is counted as a fraction of full-capacity income, this fraction also may change through time. This occurs because the *ex-ante* propensity to save may change: if it increases, the fraction increases, and vice versa. But, what is more interesting, a *demand effect* and *supply effect* will influence this fraction. As a developing country grows, it is likely that the increasingly complex production apparatus will require relatively more complex inputs. This is the demand effect. If, for instance, the need for input imports is smaller in agriculture than in manufacturing, a more rapid growth in the latter will lead to such an increase in the fraction; a fall in capacity would make the demand effect work in the opposite direction.

Capacity changes are also likely to affect the possibilities of producing domestically goods that, in the preceding period, qualified as input imports. This is the supply effect. Capacity growth will most certainly be associated with a positive supply effect. The supply effect would counteract the demand effect. If the two effects balance each other exactly, and the propensity to save is constant, there would be no changes in the required input-imports full-capacity income fraction. If the supply effect is stronger, the fraction will fall. This fall is of the greatest significance, since it is the only way in which a developing country may, eventually, escape the situation that warrants the reformulation of trade theory with which the present analysis is concerned.

However, as long as there is a definite need for input imports and the required amount is not secured, there will be *internal disequilibrium*. As can be seen, internal balance is defined here not only as the full utilization of existing capacity but as this *plus* the full utilization of the growth potential. This more ambitious definition is chosen because it highlights the special role that trade plays in the growth process—a role of potential superengine that it does not play in conventional theory.

A Diagrammatic Illustration

Figure 1 presents the factor-proportions problem with which the present analysis is concerned. On the horizontal axis, we measure operation imports (M_O) and on the vertical axis domestic factors, or rather the flow of services out of existing productive capacity (C). The substitutability between the two types of factors is assumed to be zero, an assumption that is laid down in the right-angled isoquants. If OB measures the potential maximum volume of services from existing domestic factors ($\overline{C}$), and if the actual flow of operating imports (M_O) were equal only to BA, there would be unused domestic factors of a quantity represented by BE. The distance AP then indicates the additional amount of operating imports needed for existing domestic factors to be fully utilized, and OS is the total amount of operation imports needed (M_O^+ or $p\overline{C}$). The fraction p is thus equal to OS/OB.

This is a direct adaptation of the Eckaus diagram. However, it is possible to modify the diagram to show more clearly the relationship between operation imports and domestic factor utilization. The ground will also be prepared for a diagrammatic technique that will make possible the introduction of changes in capacity over time as related to different levels of input imports per time unit.

In Figure 2, the degree of utilization of existing capacity ($C/\overline{C}$) is measured on the vertical axis. On the horizontal axis, operation imports (M_O) are measured. In this space, a function can be drawn. This function (OPV) shows how capacity use will vary with the amount of operation imports. If input imports are increased beyond a certain magnitude (corresponding to point P, i.e., OS), there will be no further increase in the use of existing capacity

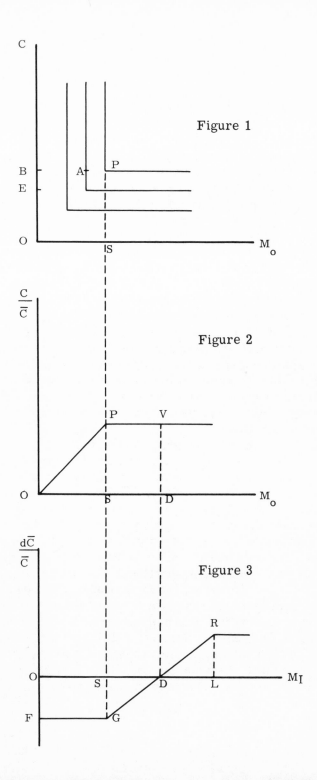

Figure 1

Figure 2

Figure 3

since it is already fully employed. Thus, the OS quantity of imports of operation inputs is equal to M_O^+. To the right of P the function will be horizontal. The section OP is analytically more interesting. This part of the function is the locus of those points on the network of underlying isoquants, where, at given levels of input imports, an increase in the use of existing domestic factors would not serve any useful purpose because it would not increase production. From this, it is evident that there is a close relationship between Figures 1 and 2. The function in Figure 2 could be developed from Figure 1 by connecting the angles in the isoquants. Point P in the two figures is thus the same point, and the quantity OS of operation imports is the same. From the method of deriving the section OP, it is clear that it is an isocline,[10] and that it is the particular isocline that connects all the points on the isoquants where the marginal productivity of domestic factors is zero. This particular isocline is also the expansion path, for, in this model, the price, or at least the shadow price, of domestic factors in relation to the price of input imports will be zero as long as the amount of input imports is smaller than the amount corresponding to P.

As to the particular shape of the function between O and P, this depends upon what further assumption is made concerning the effects of variations in input imports, i.e., whether they will result in proportional changes in capacity use or not. It is, for instance, possible to argue that a zero level of input imports would not preclude some use of domestic factors; furthermore, it can be claimed that successive additions to input imports will produce declining proportional increases in capacity use up to the point P, where further additions would result in zero increases in capacity use. The function would then have a positive intercept on the vertical axis and rise at a decreasing rate. This shape of the function would imply a decreasing leverage on capacity use. It is also possible to assume that increases in input imports have a proportional leverage on capacity use up to the maximum point *P*. *OP* would, in this case, have unitary elasticity and would be a straight line from the origin to *P*. In fact, the section *OP* can probably have any shape, subject to the restriction that it must be rising and that *O* can hardly lie to the right of the origin. The factors determining the actual shape of *OP* will be (1) differences in factor-combination requirements between industries and the relative importance of the industries in the economy at different degrees of capacity use and (2) changes in the marginal productivity (marginal leverage on capacity use) of operation imports within each industry. If it is assumed that the combination requirement is fixed within each industry, irrespective of degree of capacity use, and that it is the same in all industries (or that the weight of the various industries in total output is constant as the degree of capacity use changes), the section *OP* will be a straight line from the origin. It is under this assumption that Figure 2 has been drawn.

This kind of diagram cannot show, however, the effects of reinvestment and expansion imports on growth. For this purpose, Figure 3 has been constructed, a diagram that can be used to sum up the reasoning so far and provide a framework for the subsequent analysis. On the vertical axis, the percentage change in capacity per unit of time is indicated (thus, we do not measure $C/\bar{C}$ as in Figure 2, but $d\bar{C}/\bar{C}$), and on the horizontal axis, input imports per unit of time.

Now, if there is an actual quantity of input imports that equals maintenance imports—what is needed to maintain operations and the size of existing capacity— there will be no change in capacity. This is true, at least, if it is assumed that a developing country wants to cover its need for capacity imports before making any expansion imports. The assumption that a developing country prefers to use existing capacity before expanding capacity is plausible.[11] Thus, this amount of input imports corresponds to a point on the horizontal axis at a distance from the origin equal to the value of maintenance imports. In Figure 3, this is point *D*.

If input imports are below D, there will be a decline in capacity. This is so, at least, if it is assumed that a country, when facing this kind of choice, reduces reinvestment imports rather than operation imports. This seems an appropriate assumption, for there is no attraction in reinvesting in capacity for which there are no operation imports and which thus stand idle. It is possible that cutting down operation imports to *some* industries is preferable, in order to keep up reinvestment imports to *other* industries.[12] But, in sectors that do not obtain sufficient allotments of operation imports, there can hardly be any reason for not permitting capital equipment to deteriorate, thereby decreasing total capacity. Thus, if input imports are smaller than D, capacity will fall. If it is assumed, as in Figure 3, that all reinvestment imports will be eliminated before there is any curtailment of operation imports, the decline in the function will be concentrated to a segment GD corresponding to a need per time period of reinvestment imports, equal to SD. Any further decline in input imports below S would not reduce capacity, but would lead to a decline in the utilization of existing capacity through insufficient operation imports. Thus, the quantity OS of input imports is the same as in Figures 1 and 2. Since there is no change in capacity, but only in capacity use, this segment (GF) of the function will be horizontal. If, instead, there is a parallel decline in both reinvestment and operation imports as input imports fall below D, the decline in the function will not be concentrated to the segment GD, but will spread out over the whole FD part of the function. In both cases, however, the function would end at the same point on the vertical axis (F), the numerical value of which will depend upon the depreciation period and the length of the time unit with which we work. If the time unit is one year and the depreciation period ten years, the point F would correspond to a change in capacity of −10 per cent.

If input imports exceed D, there will be a positive rate of growth of capacity, as there is now room for expansion imports, too. However, further increases in input

imports will not bring about further increases in the
capacity growth rate when there are no further additions
to domestic factors to be employed by additional expansion
imports. The point where this stage is reached—whether
or not it represents a socially acceptable state—is R,
corresponding to expansion imports equal to DL. The
function can rise above this point, only if there are
capital imports supplementing scarce domestic resources. For input imports smaller than those corresponding to R, there will be a frustration of additions or
potential additions to domestic factors.

The growth function in Figure 3 may change position
through time, although retaining its general properties.
In fact, it *must* change position, except in the case of
pure coincidence, as soon as the actual rate of growth
is not zero. This is so because in absolute terms, the
need for input imports changes when capacity changes.
An increase in capacity increases the need for all categories of input imports, thus moving the whole function
to the right. A decline in capacity has the opposite effect.

The fact that the values assumed by the dependent
variable in the diagram change the position of the function—except in the special case of zero growth—is a
serious disadvantage, which limits the use of the diagram
to a one-period analysis. This disadvantage has been
temporarily accepted in constructing Figure 3 in order
to be able to develop that figure from Figure 2, which, in
turn, represented a development of Figure 1. However,
this disadvantage can be overcome by measuring input
imports on the horizontal axis, not in absolute figures,
but as a fraction of the full-capacity flow of services
from existing capacity, i.e., $M_I/\overline{Y}$. When this fraction is
so high that there is full-capacity use and no frustration of
savings, i.e., when it equals $(p+ms_p)$—as $M_I^+ = \overline{Y}(p+ms_p)$,
so $M_I^+/\overline{Y} = (p+ms_p)$—the function will reach its maximum
value for percentage growth of capacity. When the fraction
is between p and $(p+ms_p)$, there will be a frustration of
savings, and if it is so low that not even full reinvestment

imports can be secured, there will be such a frustration of savings that the rate of growth in capacity will be negative. If the fraction is reduced to p, there can be assumed to be no reinvestment imports, and the capacity decline will have reached its maximum value. Further reductions in the fraction will reduce capacity utilization and will not cause any decrease in the rate of capacity reduction.

Thus, it is obvious that the function has the same properties as the function in Figure 3. However, this way of expressing it has a marked advantage. If, in one period, there is some change in productive capacity and thus change in the *absolute amounts* of required imports for operation, reinvestment, and expansion purposes, the *fraction* of these amounts in relation to capacity need not change. This diagram could thus be used for a multiperiod analysis.

In Figure 3a, this modification has been introduced. The horizontal axis measures the fraction of input imports in relation to full-capacity income, instead of input imports in absolute terms. In order to relate Figure 2 to this modified version of Figure 3, the same kind of change has been made on the horizontal axis of Figure 2a. This, too, represents an improvement on Figure 2, for, if operation imports are measured in absolute terms on the horizontal axis, the function will change from period to period for the same reason that point G will change position in Figure 3.

If there is a fixed absolute volume of input imports, point D in Figure 3a represents a stable equilibrium. This is so because, if the given import level is such that the initial fraction is below D, the fraction will rise, for the denominator falls while the numerator is—by assumption—constant. This increase in the fraction will be arrested only when the fraction is so high that there is no further decrease in capacity, i.e., at D. Applying the same reasoning to the case with an initial fraction higher than D, it will be seen that there will be a process leading to a fall in the fraction to its value at D.[13] This argument means that if a country is to succeed in main-

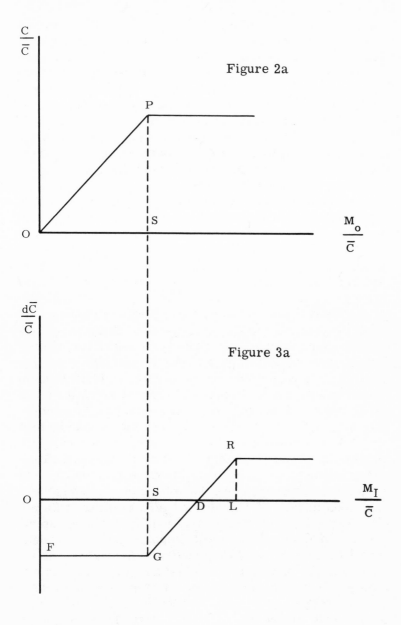

Figure 2a

Figure 3a

taining a fraction so high that there is full utilization of
the growth potential, *there must be a steady increase in
the absolute value of input imports.* It also has important
implications for a developing country with volatile foreign-exchange earnings. The foreign-exchange reserves
will here have an important function to fill as an instrument to prevent overinvestment in capacity during periods
with an ample supply of foreign exchange—capacity for
which there will be insufficient operation imports during
periods with a low supply of foreign exchange.[14]

However, even the function in Figure 3a may change
position and shape through time, which may represent an
escape from the requirement of ever increasing input
imports to maintain growth. The function may change since
the fraction of required input imports may change; however, this would be due to changes not in the dependent
variable, as in Figure 3, but in the parameters and con-
stants.

As we pointed out before embarking on this diagrammatic exposition, continued growth is likely to imply a
supply effect, leading to the increased possibility of producing domestically inputs that formerly had to be imported. Thus does a developing country eventually become
an advanced country, to the conditions of which the trade
theory here formulated is not applicable. The supply effect causes a gradual relaxation of all the various factors
that inhibit growth in an underdeveloped country. With
increasing production, this effect will tend to shift the
function to the left, but to do this the supply effect must
be strong enough to more than offset the demand effect.
The consequence of the demand effect is that, with increasing industrial complexity, relatively more capital
goods which qualify as input imports may be needed,
thereby tending to shift the function to the right.

Finally, it should be noted that an increase in the *ex-
ante* propensity to save would move the point R in a northeastern direction, i.e., the function would flatten out at a
higher rate of growth. The reverse would happen in the
case of a decrease.

The Significance of the Factor-Proportions Problem

When there is limited substitutability between domestic factors and input imports, a new element must be brought into the analysis of the role of trade. For trade will no longer affect income through the allocation of fully employed resources, but through a *leverage effect* on capacity use and capacity growth.

This is an important difference, but its significance should not be misunderstood. Not only developing countries but also industrially advanced countries face factor-proportions problems in the form of rigid import requirements to maintain production; factor-proportions analysis is thus at least somewhat applicable to advanced countries. Yet its significance here is limited. In spite of factor-proportions problems, conventional theory seems applicable to advanced countries. Some additional consideration must thus be introduced into the analysis to warrant any far-reaching reformulation of the conventional theory. However, it may first be used to explore how the factor-proportions analysis is extended to advanced countries, whether those with market economies or those with centrally planned economies.

In advanced market economies, it is evident that some inputs are virtually impossible to produce domestically. The only difference in this respect between advanced countries and developing countries is in the range of input imports required. Generally speaking, the advanced countries need only some primary commodities; their requirements are thus limited to operation imports, whereas reinvestment and expansion goods can be produced at home (even if for reasons of allocative efficiency they happen to be imported). (However, after World War II, the range of input imports into the devastated European economies was temporarily broadened to include investment goods.) In some countries, the need for operation imports has been conspicuous enough to have been explicitly noted—the United Kingdom, and Japan, for instance. In discussions on the applied level, it is frequently pointed out that the gains from trade for these countries are "extremely high"—comments that must reflect awareness of the fact that trade for these countries solves a pressing factor-proportions problem.

Centrally planned economies, typified by the Soviet Union, try to avoid an import dependence—i.e., try to escape facing, at times of external political pressure, a factor-proportions problem of the type facing the United Kingdom. They pursue a policy of autarky, instead of participation in the international division of labor.[15] Natural-resource endowments within the Communist bloc have been rich enough to permit the production of virtually all primary commodities in sufficient quantities.

But these countries are exposed to a different kind of factor-proportions problem. In a planned economy, there are bound to be discrepancies between output and input requirements—gaps between domestic output and input goals in the material balances. When there have been such discrepancies, whether foreseen at the planning stage or the result of changes or deficiencies in plans, these "bottlenecks," which are nothing but factor-proportions problems, have been solved through imports. It would have been too expensive to do otherwise, since this would have required more than just forgoing some gains from a superior allocation of resources: through a negative leverage effect, it would have left some existing capacity temporarily idle until resources could be reallocated and would have thereby slowed down the growth rate. Furthermore, to trade in these situations need not represent a breach with the principle of autarky. By accepting the costs of developing all sectors of the economy, irrespective of comparative disadvantages, and thereby avoiding permanent factor-proportions problems like those of the United Kingdom, the Soviet Union faces only *ad hoc* factor-proportions problems to be solved through *ad hoc* imports. This also means that—contrary to the situation in the United Kingdom, for instance—Soviet input imports consist of investment goods. Through the import of investment goods, the Soviet Union may be said to trade to reach a higher level of autarky.[16]

There are thus interesting differences in the factor-proportions problems that the Soviet Union, on the one hand, and countries like the United Kingdom and Japan, on the other, are solving through trade. The latter solve factor-proportions problems almost incidentally, as a consequence of their emphasis on allocation and their participation in a permanent international division of labor. The Soviet Union, however, explicitly solves factor-proportions problems and neglects allocation rewards through trading only in situations where such problems arise. Thus, although a trade theory in terms of factor-proportions problems may throw some light on the trade situation of countries like the United Kingdom and Japan, it seems more pertinent to the understanding of the role of trade in the Soviet Union.

Still, even if such an analysis told us something about the size of the gains from trade and could shed some light on the foreign-trade situation of certain countries, it would not in itself necessitate any important modification of the conventional international trade theory. The factor-proportions problem can be fitted into this theory, with its solution being regarded as a special case where the re-allocation gains are extreme. Thus, the emphasis that has been given here to this aspect would hardly be war-ranted unless some further observation was added to the analysis, which, in combination with the import minimum, would require a more dramatic departure from conven-tional theory. Such an observation will, in fact, be advanced and, in all its simplicity, will necessitate an extensive reformulation of trade theory and trade policy if they are to be applicable to developing countries. The argument in question is that *in developing countries it may not, in fact, be possible to solve the factor-proportions problem through trade.* The reason for this is the existence of an *export maximum.* Thus, it may be impossible to transform domestic factors of production into certain products re-

quired for operation and expansion purposes, *both directly*
through domestic production and *indirectly* through exports.

The Export Maximum

According to conventional theory and its main building
block, the theory of comparative advantage, there can be
no particular export maximum causing a balance-of -pay-
ments problem. A country can export those goods in the
production of which it has a relative advantage. Such an
advantage exists when the sacrifice of production factors
for the manufacture of export goods is smaller than it
would be for the production of substitutes for imports. As
long as there are such differences, there is scope for
trade, and a country can always export what it is relatively
best suited to produce. The decisive element, according to
the comparative-cost doctrine, is relative differences in
productivities. The general levels of absolute productivity
are of no concern in this context.

Of course, it is realized that the exports of any country,
including underdeveloped ones, can be arrested by inappropriate expenditure policies. In fact, only when its expenditure policy is geared to the maintenance of external
equilibrium can a country export all those goods in the production of which it has a comparative advantage. However,
conventional trade theory tells us that in the case of a
deficit, it is always economically possible, even if sometimes politically difficult, to tighten up the expenditure
policy so as to reduce imports and to make the country
capable of actually exporting such goods. On the basis of
this argument, monetary problems can be disregarded in
pure theory, where the simultaneous existence of internal
equilibrium and external equilibrium is assumed.

Similarly, according to conventional trade theory,
trade obstacles abroad may impede the exports of any
country, including underdeveloped ones, but such obstacles, by leading to a deterioration in the terms of trade,

would also reduce imports; they would thus not create any external disequilibrium. Again, this is on the assumption that the country adjusts its expenditure policies to lower income levels resulting from deteriorated terms of trade. Thus, according to the comparative-cost doctrine, there can be no obstacle, other than faulty expenditure policies, to the maintenance of an export level sufficiently high to ensure external balance concurrently with internal balance. It is this tenet that will be criticized presently.

The *welfare* implications of the comparative-cost doctrine—that participation in international trade on the basis of comparative cost differences is advantageous—have, of course, often been exposed to criticism. It has been argued that the comparative-cost doctrine is useless as a guide to specialization through time. Relative prices may change both exogenously and, more interestingly, through the very pattern of specialization of investment that is being selected. For underdeveloped countries, it has, in fact, been maintained that the comparative-cost doctrine is not only useless but outright dangerous as a basis for investment decisions: it is argued that its application would dictate a pattern of trade which would make permanent a growth-hampering structure of production. The usefulness of comparative costs as a guide to specialization at a given time has also been questioned. (One instance of such criticism is the Manoilesco-Hagen case already referred to, but this kind of criticism is better seen as an argument for the introduction of certain corrective measures before actual prices reflect true comparative costs and before they can be allowed to determine the pattern of specialization.[17])

Even if the welfare aspects of the comparative-cost doctrine have been criticized, and criticized severely, it is noteworthy that its implications as to the possibilities of establishing *external balance* have never been attacked, but are, indeed, considered self-evident. Yet this part of the doctrine is based on an implicit assumption the nature of which never seems to have attracted any attention: that the *general level of absolute productivity is high enough to allow the production of a sufficient amount of those goods which are, in fact, demanded abroad.* This condition might not in fact be met.

Perhaps it seems surprising that one can raise this objection against the comparative-cost doctrine. After all, the doctrine was originally developed to show that even if the real costs of one country were above those of other countries in all industries (cf. Great Britain in relation to Portugal in the Ricardian example), this country would nonetheless be capable of participating in international trade. But low absolute productivities can certainly be of concern. To begin with, there is the low productivity in those inputs the domestic production of which is ruled out and which thus have to be imported to ensure internal balance. This means that, in order to establish concurrent external and internal balance, the adjustment burden is shifted over to export expansion rather than import contraction. But—and this is the central problem—this export expansion might be limited by the absolute productivity being so low that the value added in the production of exports was negative; i.e., requirement of input imports for export production might demand more foreign exchange than the exports eventually yield.

In order to discuss this possibility in greater detail and to determine its relevance for developing countries, it is first necessary to formulate a theory of the structure of relative prices.

The relative price structure for *manufactures* can be determined by the theory of "representative demand."[18] According to this theory, a country is most efficient in the manufacture of goods that fit into the economic structure of the domestic market. Inventors, innovators, and entrepreneurs are stimulated by home demand. They are aware of domestic needs and are in sufficiently good contact with the market to be able to develop the products that will satisfy them. Then, the more the demand for a particular product is typical of the economic structure of one particular country compared with other countries, the lower the relative price of this product is likely to be in that country. *The production function for it will be more advantageous in that country.* For goods not typical of the domestic demand structure, the production function will be disadvantageous.

Now the chief determinant of the demand structure in a country is the per-capita income level, and there are, thus, great differences in demand structures between advanced and developing countries. These differences mean that goods in demand in advanced countries are atypical for the economic structure of developing countries; their production functions will be disadvantageous in the latter countries. Goods that developing countries are particularly adept at producing are, on the other hand, not demanded in the advanced countries.

Owing to lack of foreign demand, the developing countries therefore cannot export those manufactures they are most efficient at producing. Generally speaking, they are reduced to trying to export manufactures with which they are unfamiliar to markets of which they have no experience.

To illustrate the marketing problems that may arise and the general effects of unfamiliarity with the products demanded in advanced countries, we might refer to a study made by the Swedish Importers' and Wholesalers' Organization on the particular difficulties encountered in importing from the underdeveloped countries.[19] The findings can be summarized in the following way. There is a lack of confidence in the financial position and reliability of exporters in underdeveloped countries: the exporters regularly ask for payment under confirmed letters of credit but often do not accept the right of reclamation. Pricing policies do not recognize the need for especially low prices during the introductory stage of a product. The technical norms and standards do not suit the rigorous requirements of the advanced countries or, at least, the special needs of particular countries (especially small countries like Sweden). Finish, patterns, colors, and packaging could be made more attractive. Deliveries are often not according to samples. Delivery dates are not kept, and continuity in deliveries is not good enough. Finally, the information abroad of the existence of potential export products is poor.[20]

These criticisms may help to explain the "export fatalism" that easily arises in developing countries as a result of unsuccessful attempts to enter foreign markets without a sufficient understanding of their characteristics. The obstacles to exporting unfamiliar products to unfamiliar markets may also appear in the form of what has been referred to as negative value added. This is true for a combination of reasons. First, the need for input imports for such production is likely to be particularly pronounced: in order to fulfill the requirements of high qualitative standards, both in production and marketing, and of mass production and mass marketing, foreign-exchange expenditures on imported machinery and foreign sales costs abroad will be high. Second, unfamiliarity with the production and with the markets is likely to increase the risk that these input imports will be wasted, to the extent that the value added actually becomes negative.

In the original formulation of the comparative-cost doctrine, the possibility of too low an absolute productivity has been overlooked, evidently because it was taken for granted that the goods entering into international trade were all produced in the pretrade situation. In the Ricardian example, the United Kingdom had a lower productivity than Portugal both in wine and clothing, but she produced both goods in the pretrade situation. If, before trade is opened up, a low-productivity country actually produces the whole range of goods that are produced and demanded in other countries, it is obvious that they do so at a productivity level that is high enough at least to permit subsistence factor rewards. In that case, goods that are at a comparative advantage, in the sense that they would have to be exported to pay for imports, can, in fact, be exported. In more technical terms, the Hawkins-Simon condition is assumed to be fulfilled.

The subsequent addition of the factor-proportions

theory, providing a systematic explanation of the pattern of comparative advantages, and based on the assumption that production functions are the same in all countries, eliminated for good any problems of absolute advantages. If a country produces anything at all, it *must* be able to export the goods in the production of which it has an advantage compared with the goods it imports. In other words, the comparative-cost doctrine can be applied without reservation. Developing countries have a comparative advantage and, assuming appropriate expenditure policies, have no export difficulties regarding all those products that are more labor-intensive than the import products. External balance would thus be ensured.

But even if there is a limitation on the exports of manufactures in the form of low absolute productivity, the situation with respect to *primary products* is likely to be different. Differences in production functions render the differences in factor proportions irrelevant for the pattern of trade in manufactured goods; but factor proportions are necessarily of great significance for the exportability of primary products. If a developing country has an abundant supply of some natural resource, it is unlikely that low productivity in exploiting this resource will prevent the export of products derived from it. Still, although a developing country may be able to export various primary products, there can be an upper limit to such exports, too. This is in conformity with conventional theory, where an export maximum for individual products—set either by inelastic foreign demand or by decreasing marginal productivity or, as is most likely, by a combination of the two—is, of course, recognized.

When discussing a maximum for primary-commodity exports of developing countries set by inelastic foreign demand, it is important to determine which foreign-demand curves a developing country has to reckon. Should one look at the world-demand curve or the demand curve facing a particular developing country? If a country does not have 100 per cent of the world market, these two

curves will differ; and the latter will be more elastic at
each price than the former curve. First, a reduction in
price will, from the point of view of the individual country, increase demand for the product, not only by the
amount by which world demand increases, but also by the
amount by which the supply of the rest of the world decreases. Second, when the demand elasticity for an individual country is calculated, change in demand is related to a smaller original quantity—i.e., the quantity
supplied by this particular country at the original
price—than the one used when calculating world-demand
elasticity.[21] However, what is ultimately interesting is the
impact on the developing countries in the aggregate.
Therefore, it seems reasonable to base estimates of the
export maximum on the less elastic demand curve facing
the group—all the more so as independent action by one
country is likely to lead to retaliation.

The differences in international competitiveness between primary products and manufactures create one
more problem in the expansion of exports from developing
countries, one that may arise even if there were a positive value added in the production of some manufactures
for exports. The problem is that, for a producer of manufactures to be competitive on the advanced export markets
and at the same time able to pay at least subsistence
factor rewards in domestic currency, the price of foreign
exchange must be made very high. The exchange rate must
be high, that is, in relation to what would be required to
market the primary products. And this high exchange rate
may lead to a supply of primary products so large that,
owing to inelastic foreign demand, there is a net loss in
the total supply of foreign exchange. The height to which
the exchange rate would have to go would, of course, depend upon the productivity level in manufacturing, but it
would also be contingent upon the extent to which the final
products consist of input imports. The higher this percentage, the higher the exchange rate must be. If there is
a negative value added in the manufacture of products des-
tined for foreign markets, no exchange rate at all can
make the products exportable. If increases in the exchange

rate push up subsistence factor rewards in domestic currency, the devaluation must be taken still further. In this case, the side effects of the exchange-rate policy would give rise to a variety of economic policy problems. However, irrespective of these considerations, the higher the exchange rate must be, the greater the risks that other export products from more productive sectors will earn less foreign exchange—so much less that the total supply is negatively affected.

In conclusion, therefore, it must be recognized that in developing countries, there may be an export maximum for both manufactures and primary commodities. With the former, the maximum is due to domestic-supply conditions such that the goods cannot be produced and exported. The fact that the domestic supply conditions for certain goods are more advantageous than the domestic supply conditions are for input imports, so that the first-mentioned goods show a comparative advantage in the sense of conventional doctrine, does not turn those goods into exportables. Only relatively simple manufactures are likely to be exportable, and then by countries that have a comparatively developed modern sector. As for primary products, it should be remembered that underdeveloped countries are "primary-producing countries," not because they produce and export more primary commodities than advanced countries, but because they export virtually *only* such goods. For these exports, the export maximum is determined by the maximum for each of the individual commodities.

There is great importance in having a theory which allows export difficulties independent of internal policies. It is made possible by the theory of representative demand, which also, and equally significantly, shows that a developing country must somehow pass through a stage of development plagued by foreign trade difficulties, in order to become able to export manufactures. Without such a theory, discussions of a "foreign-exchange constraint" amount to nothing more than a string of arguments based on a peculiar assumption in direct conflict with the comparative-cost theory.

The Foreign-Exchange Gap

In developing countries, an import minimum and an export maximum will exist simultaneously. *The export maximum may be too low for the import minimum to be covered.* In this case, the country is said to face an acute foreign-exchange gap. If, on the other hand, the export maximum covers the import minimum, the foreign-exchange gap is a potential gap because, as long as the import minimum and the export maximum exist, an acute foreign-exchange gap may emerge. In fact, a developing country may be expected to move back and forth between potential and acute foreign-exchange-gap situations. The position in which it will actually find itself at any one time will depend upon a variety of circumstances. In cases where there is growth, a constant ratio of required input imports to income or capacity would necessitate increasing absolute input imports, while exports might not be rising. One must also consider the interaction between the supply and demand effects, changing the ratio of required input imports to capacity as income and capacity grow. Charges for servicing foreign loans and investments, a special category of input imports for operation purposes, also change through time. Finally, the terms of trade of commodity exports are volatile. (To argue whether or not they have deteriorated through a given period is somewhat misleading. This is a problem in price theory, possibly with some moral overtones. The more relevant aspect in this context is whether or not the terms of trade are sufficiently favorable to prevent the foreign-exchange gap from becoming acute.)

A developing country will not solve the problem of a foreign-exchange gap conclusively, whether the gap is acute or potential, until there is no particular limit to industrial exports. Applying the theory of representative demand as an "expectational theory of comparative advantage," we may conclude that this situation will occur when the country is virtually an advanced country. Countries like the United Kingdom and Japan, with a pronounced import minimum, do not face a foreign-exchange gap because they have no particular export maximum. In theoretical model building, an export maximum is probably a prerequisite for paying attention to an import minimum. When, after World War II, the European countries faced an export maximum, due to war damages inflicted on the production apparatus, and this maximum was definitely too low for the import minimum to be covered (i.e., an acute foreign-exchange gap opened up), the import minimum was clearly noticed. In this situation, a flourishing "dollar shortage" discussion began. The foreign-exchange-gap analysis has substantial bearing on that discussion and on the problem underlying it. It could serve as an unconventional explanation of the dollar shortage. It could also be used to predict that the dollar shortage would disappear once the export maximum had been eliminated and that then the balance-of-payments relationships of these countries could again be analyzed with the help of conventional theory.

In the ensuing analysis, emphasis will be on the implications of acute foreign-exchange gaps, defined as *the difference between the need for foreign exchange for input imports and the amount of foreign exchange available for such imports from current-account transactions and autonomous capital movements, assuming the pursuance of optimum expenditure policies and commercial policies formulated on the basis of conventional trade theory.*

Although this definition contains various elements that should be clear from the preceding discussion, it may be appropriate to restate some of them here.

First, it is assumed that conventional commercial policies are being pursued. An acute foreign-exchange gap could possibly be hidden by various kinds of commercial-policy controls aiming at the elimination of non-input imports or at the stimulation of exports. According to conventional theory, such measures are not necessary to establish external equilibrium and internal equilibrium. All controls—other than those recognized in conventional doctrine—are therefore regarded, by definition, as incom-

patible with equilibrium. Thus, it is appropriate to define
an acute foreign-exchange gap as one that would emerge
under a conventional commercial policy.

Second, it is assumed that optimum expenditure policies are being pursued; i.e., that current-account earnings
are not reduced through the diversion of exportables and
that imports of non-inputs are not inflated through overexpenditure. The possibility of inept expenditure policies
means that the existence of an actual balance-of-payments
deficit is not a conclusive sign that a country is facing
a foreign-exchange gap. It could also mean that only part
of an actual deficit constitutes a true foreign-exchange
gap.

It should be noted, however, that assuming the pursuit
of optimum expenditure policies does not rule out the
possibility that there are certain non-input imports, particularly as the pursuit of conventional commercial policies is simultaneously assumed. This possibility remains
because a combination of expenditure cuts and expenditure
shifts would affect different import commodities differently. Before all non-input imports have been eliminated,
it might well have created internal imbalance in other
ways, e.g., through a deficiency of Keynesian effective
demand or of incentives. Furthermore, considering the
export structure of developing countries and the assumption of conventional commercial policies, general expenditure policies of a harsh nature may well lead to a proportionally greater reduction in exports than in non-input
imports. In view of the leverage effects of input imports,
one may well ask why any non-input imports would be demanded before the import minimum has been covered. It
must be remembered that the benefits of input imports
are, to a great extent, social rather than private, i.e., they
create external economies. But it should be observed that,
even if there were no non-input imports under optimum
expenditure policies, foreign-exchange gaps may, of
course, exist. All that would be needed is for the export
maximum (including autonomous capital inflows) to exceed
the import minimum.

Finally, accommodating, or compensatory, capital movements to cover the import minimum are *not* counted on the supply side when calculating the foreign-exchange gap.

It is evident from the definition of the foreign-exchange gap that it appears on the "program balance of payments." Machlup, who introduced this concept, defined a deficit on a program balance of payments in the following way: "A dollar deficit in a country's programme balance of payments may be defined as an excess of dollar amounts needed or desired for some specified purposes (assumed to be important with reference to some accepted standards) over the dollar amounts expected to become available from regular sources."[22] Whether or not a foreign-exchange gap of a developing country will be reflected in a gap on the accounting balance of payments is a question to be discussed later, in connection with the analysis of the commercial policy of countries facing foreign-exchange gaps. Within the analytical framework being developed, however, a foreign-exchange gap on the program balance of payments cannot be treated as lightly as it was by Machlup. According to Machlup, who was working with conventional balance-of-payments theory, a deficit on the program balance of payments simply reflects inappropriate expenditure policies and import needs formulated as wishful thinking. But, as already stressed, our position is that such a deficit can exist in spite of optimum balance-of-payments policies and with import needs defined in terms of what is required for internal balance.

Thus, a foreign-exchange gap on the program balance, which is not reflected in a deficit on the accounting balance, too, must mean that *internal disequilibrium is substituted for external disequilibrium*. In conclusion: if $M_I^+ = M_I > X$, there will be external disequilibrium but internal equilibrium; if $M_I^+ > M_I = X$, there will be external equilibrium but internal disequilibrium; if $M_I^+ > M_I > X$, there will be external and internal disequilibrium simultaneously.

The existence of a foreign-exchange gap, whether acute

or potential, thus means that the balance-of-payments adjustment measures do not have the same efficiency as when they are applied in advanced countries. This is, of course, most noticeable if the foreign-exchange gap is acute. Such a gap is not, in the case of an external deficit, a reflection of overambition and the overexertion of domestic resources. Nor is it, in the case of internal disequilibrium, with underutilization and frustration of domestic resources, the manifestation of insufficient effective demand, as it would be in Keynesian theory. Instead, the truth is that none of the expenditure shifters and expenditure adjusters that make up the conventional balance-of-payments policy outfit is effective. For instance, whatever the exchange rate and income level, exchange earnings cannot be increased beyond the export maximum and foreign-exchange requirements cannot be decreased below the import minimum.[23]

Such a disequilibrium cannot exist in conventional balance-of-payments theory. Advanced countries are, under modern conditions, sometimes said to find themselves in a "disequilibrium system."[24] But this is so because it is politically difficult to bring about the appropriate corrective measures. A developing country may also experience political difficulties in applying optimum expenditure policies, but—and this is what needs emphasis—to the extent that there is an acute foreign-exchange gap, this disequilibrium could not be corrected even if it were politically feasible to pursue optimum expenditure policies.

These observations on the impotence of expenditure policies *do not,* however, mean that such policies are indifferent. On the contrary. To begin with, the situation could certainly be worsened by suboptimal expenditure policies, even if it could not be made perfect through optimum expenditure policies. Furthermore, balance-of-payments adjustment measures are surely effective in the sense that they can always be used to establish external equilibrium. Even if exchange-rate and income changes cannot increase exports beyond their maximum, they can certainly reduce imports below the *required* level. The crucial point is that this would mean a reduction in input imports, and that, in this way, internal disequilibrium would be substituted for the external inbalance.

To highlight the important differences between conventional theory and the foreign-exchange-gap theory, it might be interesting to relate the latter to the Keynesian accounting identities. It should then be observed that the following equilibrium conditions of income determination, being a matter of definitions, must of course hold in the foreign-exchange-gap analysis, as well as under conventional circumstances:

$$X - M = Y - E = S - I_d = I_f,$$

where X = exports, M = imports, Y = national income, E = aggregate expenditure, S = savings, I_d = domestic investments, and I_f = investment abroad (i.e., when negative this means foreign disinvestment).

The fact that $M = X$ if I_f represents zero just means that the conventional adjustment mechanism works to the extent that external equilibrium can always be assured; however, when the foreign-exchange gap is acute, this must be at the expense of internal equilibrium. It is, of course, true that there may be internal disequilibrium in Keynesian theory, too. The recognition of this possibility was, after all, one of the most characteristic innovations of Keynesian theory. However, in Keynesian theory, the existence of such a disequilibrium is only a *possibility* arising out of the rigidity of what classical economists treated as automatic self-correcting processes. A Keynesian disequilibrium can, furthermore, be avoided through the application of appropriate economic-policy measures without upsetting the external balance. As has been seen, it is here that the foreign-exchange-gap analysis differs.

Behind this difference lie important differences in the workings of the two models. Keynesian theory asserts that, if there is internal deflationary disequilibrium, effective demand can be increased through measures stimulating consumption, investment, and/or exports. The latter is particularly important, in that it should prevent external disequilibrium from emerging when domestic expenditure and income rise. According to the foreign-exchange-gap analysis, however, exports cannot be stimulated beyond their maximum; an increase in production for consumption purposes cannot be engineered if there is a lack of operation imports, and such an increase would only be, under all circumstances, a way of hiding the frustration of savings; and investment, finally, cannot be increased, owing to a lack of investment imports.

On the other hand, if there is an external deficit, Keynesian theory tells us that it could be cured through an increase in savings. According to the foreign-exchange-gap analysis, however, if the *ex-ante* propensity to save (s_p) is increased in an attempt to reduce absorption, the result would, in fact, be a *widening* of the foreign-exchange gap. This is because the amount of input imports required to utilize savings would increase while foreign-exchange earnings would not increase—assuming the pursuance of optimum expenditure policies at the outset.

Another important difference is that, according to the foreign-exchange-gap theory, an increase in imports in the form of input imports will not lead to a fall in effective demand and income domestically. It will, instead, exert a positive *leverage effect* on domestic income, either immediately, if there is a lack of operation imports that is being remedied, or eventually, if there can be a reduction in frustrated domestic investment resources.

From this analysis, it is evident that capital imports, i.e., foreign disinvestments, play a different role from the one they assume in conventional theory. There, they are treated as a *supplement* to insufficient domestic factors. Here, they represent a complement to a glut of domestic factors, making possible the purposeful use of these abundant factors. Not until an acute foreign-exchange gap has been closed will capital imports assume their other function of supplementing scarce domestic factors. The limit to their usefulness here would be set by the "capacity to absorb foreign capital."[25]

It is very interesting and important in the analytical framework suggested here to make a distinction between capital imports to be combined with available domestic factors or available additions to domestic factors and capital imports to be supplemented to domestic factors. The first kind of capital imports increases capacity use by relieving the M_0/p constraint and increases *ex-post* savings by relieving the M_i/m constraint, whereas the latter kind of capital imports supplements $s_p Y$.

These differences can be further clarified in terms of the accounting identities. According to conventional theory, an increase in foreign disinvestment must—if one assumes optimum expenditure policies—imply an increase in imports, or a fall in exports of a net total magnitude equal to the change in I_f or both. There will be no change in Y, since, under optimum expenditure policies, there will already be internal equilibrium. E will increase, however, by the amount of the change in I_f. There will, furthermore, be an increase in I_d, or a fall in S of a net total magnitude equal to the change in I_f, or both.

In terms of the foreign-exchange-gap analysis, these changes will be quite different. If optimum expenditure policies are assumed, and imports consist solely of input imports, an increase in foreign disinvestment will, when there is an acute foreign-exchange gap, lead to an increase in M equal to the change in I_f, but to no fall in X. If the foreign-exchange gap was serious enough originally to obstruct full operation imports, Y will increase. E will, under all circumstances, rise, and this increase will always exceed that in Y by an amount equal to the change in I_f. There will also be an increase in I_d. This increase can, to the extent the capital imports finance investment imports, be specified as I_f/m, i.e., the increase in foreign disinvestment will increase domestic investment by more than the foreign disinvestment. This implies—and here lies the most conspicuous difference from conventional analysis—that S will increase (and not remain stable or fall as in conventional analysis). The increase in savings will be smaller than the rise in domestic investment by the amount of the change in foreign disinvestment.

Theoretical Implications of the Foreign-Exchange Gap

The import minimum and the export maximum work as a pair of scissors that cuts deeply into the well-woven fabric of conventional trade theory. The main differences between the foreign-exchange-gap analysis and conventional theory may be summarized in the following points:

1. *The gains from trade are of a different nature.* A developing country trades to acquire inputs into which domestic factors cannot be transformed directly through domestic production. Thus, it trades to attain a multiplicative effect on its capacity use and growth, rather than to improve the allocation of existing, fully employed resources in the marginalist sense. Through this *leverage effect*, trade can be characterized as a *superengine* of growth, rather than as a mere engine of growth, as it has often been described. A developing country trades to acquire input imports equal to $Y(p + ms_p)$. This is true whether or not it is exposed to an acute foreign-exchange gap. However, if a developing country does not fill its import requirements and thus faces an acute foreign-exchange gap, the extremely attractive gains from trade tend to become exasperating, as they cannot be fully realized. Thus, the domestic factors cannot be transformed into the full variety of required inputs even indirectly through trade. Trade is, then, rather a *potential* superengine of growth. Exports become a "lagging," rather than a "leading," sector.

Advanced countries also trade to acquire input imports. For market economies, the range of input imports is limited to primary commodities (operation imports). Advanced, planned economies that try to achieve autarky are likely to find themselves facing *ad hoc* needs for all kinds of input imports. However, for advanced countries, there cannot be acute foreign-exchange gaps, and the gains can thus be fully realized. (An exception to this rule occurred in the period after World War II.)

2. The possibility of an export maximum means that the *comparative-cost doctrine has limited validity.* A developing country may not be able to export the goods in which it is most competitive, since there might be no demand for these products in advanced countries. With regard to products for which there *is* a foreign demand, the country may not be able to export enough of those goods in the production of which it has a "comparative advantage," since productivity is not high enough to support the factors involved in their production.

3. *The existing balance-of-payments theory cannot be* applied if there is a foreign-exchange gap. This is most noticeable if the foreign-exchange gap is acute. Contrary to the situation in conventional analysis, internal and external equilibrium cannot be established simultaneously. Whatever the expenditure policies, imports cannot be reduced below a certain level without causing internal, instead of external, disequilibrium; and exports cannot be stimulated as in advanced countries. Thus, a foreign-exchange gap reflected in an actual balance-of-payments deficit does not imply overabsorption of goods and services in the ordinary sense. No matter how much the absorption is reduced, the deficit cannot be removed without substituting internal disequilibrium for external.

Conventional balance-of-payments adjustment measures are, however, applicable to the extent that (*a*) suboptimal expenditure policies would aggravate the situation, and (*b*) conventional measures can be used to reduce actual imports, even if this would be at the expense of internal equilibrium.

4. *The usual kind of savings-investment equation in Keynesian and growth models must be modified.* As long as there is an acute foreign-exchange gap, it is inappropriate to use $I = S = sY$, even if this is an *ex-post* identity.

Instead, one should recognize the import constraint on investment and work with the equality $I = S = M_i/m$.

5. In countries with *an acute foreign-exchange gap, the nature of capital imports differs* from that assumed in conventional theory because capital imports do not supplement scarce domestic resources. Instead, they have the effect of increasing input imports so that M_i/m rises, thereby increasing S, so that sY approaches s_pY. These capital imports thus complement abundant domestic resources, instead of adding to scarce domestic resources. After the foreign-exchange gap has been closed, capital imports serve the usual function.

6. If external equilibrium and internal equilibrium cannot be achieved simultaneously, *the basic postulate of the pure theory of international trade is not fulfilled.* The usual division of trade theory into balance-of-payments theory and pure theory cannot be made. Balance-of-payments considerations must be brought into the analysis of structure and welfare. This means that the whole edifice of commercial-policy conclusions built into pure theory is inapplicable in trade relationships with advanced countries.

Although the emphasis in a theory of trade should naturally fall on the effects of trade, it might, nonetheless, be thought that the theory set out here neglects other important factors in the development process. But this is not the case. This trade theory instead *reflects* these other factors. For instance, such general circumstances as illiteracy, fatalism, and conventionalism, often quoted as hostile to development, affect both the size and the rigidity of the import minimum and export maximum. So does lack of entrepreneurship, much emphasized by Hirschman, at the same time that a foreign-exchange gap makes things harder for whatever entrepreneurship there is. As to capital, there is a shortage of physical capital in many developing countries; but in countries plagued by foreign-exchange gaps, this reflects a shortage of investment imports rather than of *ex-ante* savings. There is also a link with the population problem. Population growth may create "excess labor," in the sense that the entire labor force is not included among the domestic factors that could be utilized if there were sufficient operation and investment imports. Population growth can thus create a true Eckaus factor-proportions problem, underemployment in other cases being the result of a shortage of physical capital due to a lack of investment imports. Population growth is also likely to reduce per-capita incomes and, in this way, affect *ex-ante* savings. Lower per-capita incomes will also lengthen the "economic distance" to the advanced countries and thus reduce the export possibilities by producing a demand pattern that diverges more and more from that of advanced countries.

The Foreign-Exchange Gap As It Emerges in Statistics and in the Literature

Empirical proof of the existence of foreign-exchange gaps is not easy to provide. If the generalizations that have been deduced here are to be established empirically, detailed studies for a range of countries of the following phenomena would be required: (1) the substitutability between domestic inputs and certain inputs which are being imported; (2) the relationship between input imports, capacity use, investment, and growth; and (3) the effects of expenditure policies on the export potential. Such analyses cannot be made within the scope of the present study. But deductive theorizing does not take place in an empirical vacuum, and certain factual evidence is available, as well as more qualitative assessments made by economists familiar with quantitative relationships in underdeveloped countries. This supporting evidence has the additional attraction of providing an opportunity simultaneously to review those contributions for which the model presented in this chapter serves as an elaboration. The discussion attempts to answer two questions: (1) whether the import minimum and export maximum are relevant concepts, and (2) whether there are any acute foreign-exchange gaps.

As to the import minimum, it is interesting to note
that the Economic Commission for Latin America (ECLA)
estimates that the foreign-exchange component of gross
fixed investment in Latin America amounted in 1954-56
to 23 per cent, excluding any repercussions on imports
through the multiplier. As 26 per cent of gross fixed investment was made up of machinery and equipment, obviously only a very low portion of such goods could be
produced domestically. ECLA also thinks that the share
of these "investment imports" will increase over time,
because the proportion of total investment represented by
machinery and equipment is bound to rise as manufacturing industry becomes increasingly important in the
economies of these countries.[26] Information on investment and foreign-exchange requirements is also provided
in India's Third Five Year Plan.[27] The direct foreign-
exchange component is estimated to be 20 per cent of
total investment. For manufacturing industry, the figure
is as high as 40 per cent. The plan also specifies a figure
for the import need for raw materials, components, and
replacement of machinery. This need for what is now
called "maintenance imports" seems to be estimated at
some 10 per cent of nonagricultural income.

These calculations of import requirements for Latin
America and India must be understood not as trivial
ex-post observations of the import content in investment
but as *ex-ante* estimates of rock-bottom minima. Whatever the reasons for the limitations on substitutability
indicated by these estimates, substantial input-import
requirements have been specified. This would probably
also be true of other countries and regions.

But to the extent these *ex-ante* estimates are of any
relevance, it should be possible, *ex-post*, to observe a
correlation between changes through time in imports and
investment. In Diagram 1, import and investment data
for a fifteen-year period have been plotted for Latin
America. This is a region that has been exposed to substantial swings in imports, and it should be possible to
observe the effects of these savings on investment
activity. As can be seen from the technical description of

Diagram 1
Imports and Investments in Latin America, 1945–60

billions of dollars

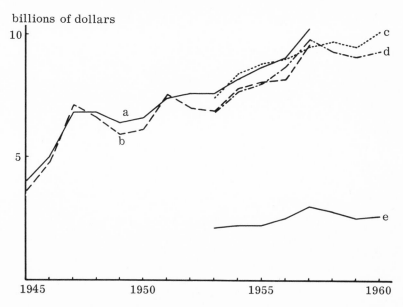

a = gross internal fixed investment, 1945-57
b = total imports of goods and services, 1945-57
c = gross domestic fixed capital formation, 1953-60
d = total imports of goods and services
e = imports of capital goods from Western industrial countries,
    1953-60

Sources: a and b: *The Latin American Common Market*, p. 54
(dollar figures in 1950 prices). c and d: U.N., *World Economic
Survey*, Vol. I, 1963, Table 3 A-2 and 3 A-1 (dollar figures in
1960 prices). e: GATT, *International Trade*, for successive
years (in current prices, adjusted to 1960 prices, using price
index for machinery in U.N., *Monthly Bulletin of Statistics*,
18:XII-XV, Special Table B [January, 1964]).

the graph, the various series are from different sources.
However, the only substantial difference is that the import
data from 1945–57 cover total imports, whereas the
figures for 1953-60 refer only to imports of "capital
goods" (SITC, Section 7 except passenger cars).
    The series move together to a high degree. If, as in

Diagram 2
Correlation Between Imports and Investments
for Latin America
(in billions of dollars at 1950 prices)

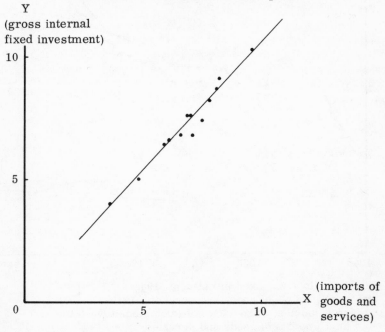

The correlation coefficient $r_{xy} = \dfrac{\Sigma (x - \overline{x})(y - \overline{y})}{\sqrt{\Sigma (x - \overline{x})^2 \, \Sigma (y - \overline{y})^2}} = 0.9793$

The equation of the regression line $y = 0.019 + 1.0567x$

Diagram 2, we run a regression equation on the 1945–57 series, the correlation coefficient will be found to be as high as 0.98. However, it must be noticed that this result is not as dramatic as might first be thought, for the test in question explores only a necessary, and not a sufficient, condition for our theory to be applicable. This is so because the causal relationship may be the reverse of that suggested here. Instead of the level of imports determining the level of investments, perhaps changes in investment, through their effects on general business activity, affect the level of imports. This reversed relationship would, indeed, conform with conventional theory, and it is thus no surprise that similar regression analyses for advanced countries also show high correlation coefficients. However, if one judges from the empirical material already furnished on the import minimum and the direct foreign-exchange component in investment, the dependent variable in developing countries seems to be investment, rather than imports. The same kind of regression analyses for developing areas other than Latin America also results in high correlation coefficients. However, owing to the inconclusiveness of the test, it is questionable whether data in addition to those furnished in Diagram 2 are of any great interest.[28]

The alleged export maximum is more difficult to illustrate statistically. All that seems possible to do, using readily available material, is to show that—in conformity with a priori arguments already put forward—underdeveloped countries, including developing countries and regions, do face special export problems. As can be seen from Table 1, manufactured exports, although they have increased both absolutely and in relation to total exports of underdeveloped countries, are still small (the increase exports may depend upon the weak prices of primary products); as a percentage of world exports of manufactures, they have shown a stable or falling tendency; it is also noteworthy that a large portion is made up of technically simple products belonging to SITC, Section 6 (base metals). As concerns total exports from underdeveloped countries to Western industrial countries, there has been an increase amounting to some 60 per cent in the twelve-year period 1953–64 and to 25 per cent during the five-year period 1960–64. This means an average annual increase considerably smaller than that of the exports of the Western industrial countries during the same period. On the whole, the increase in the exports of underdeveloped countries reflects an increase in foreign demand and not any economic-policy efforts in the underdeveloped countries. It is, of course, possible that export problems can be accounted for by faulty expenditure policies and import restrictions abroad. However,

TABLE 1

Exports from Underdeveloped Countries

Year	Total Exports to World (Billions of U.S. Dollars)	Total Exports to Western Industrial Countries (Billions of U.S. Dollars)	Manufactured Exports to Western Industrial Countries as Percentage of Total Exports to Western Industrial Countries (Excluding Australia, New Zealand, South Africa)	Manufactured Exports, Excluding Base Metals, to Western Industrial Countries as Percentage of Total Exports to Western Industrial Countries	Total Manufactured Exports as Percentage of World Manufactured Exports
1953	21.1	14.8	10.1	4.1	7.8
1954	22.1	15.4	10.4	...	7.6
1955	23.7	16.4	12.2	4.8	6.6
1956	24.9	17.5	12.0	4.6	6.4
1957	25.4	17.5	10.9	5.1	5.6
1958	24.8	17.2	9.9	5.2	5.0
1959	25.8	18.1	11.6	6.1	5.3
1960	27.4	19.0	12.6	5.8	5.5
1961	27.6	19.0	13.2	6.3	5.4
1962	28.9	20.1	13.4	7.0	5.3
1963	31.4	22.0	14.1	8.2	5.6
1964	34.0	23.9	15.5	9.2	5.4

Sources: United Nations, *Monthly Bulletin of Statistics,* 15: Special Table E (March 1961), Special Table B (April 1961); 18: Special Table C (March 1964), Special Table B (April 1964). GATT, *International Trade, 1961* (Geneva, 1962) and *International Trade, 1964* (Geneva 1965).

58

on the basis of the a priori arguments, the burden of proof seems to rest just as much on those arguing that export problems can be given a conventional explanation.

If, in order to proceed, the existence of import minima and export maxima for developing countries is tentatively accepted, the next question is to what extent the export maximum is smaller than the import minimum—i.e., how frequently and how acute are foreign-exchange gaps. Of course, whatever evidence there is of *acute* foreign-exchange gaps means that the relevance of the analytical framework *as such,* i.e., of the import minimum–export maximum concepts, is further confirmed.

To obtain an empirical answer to this question, the obvious starting point would be the actual balance-of-payments situation. It is well known that virtually all under-developed countries are exposed to balance-of-payments difficulties. (The only exceptions are the oil-producing countries, successful agricultural exporters like Thailand, and perhaps certain backward countries that are not engaged in a determined development effort.) It might be argued, however, that the statistically observable balance-of-payments difficulties could be the result of over-spending, or of trade obstacles applied by foreign countries, instead of a foreign-exchange gap.

There are, of course, a number of import restrictions in advanced countries hampering the exports of developing countries. But in the framework of conventional trade theory, these obstacles could not put any absolute limit on exports; they could only lead to a deterioration in terms of trade and make trade less attractive at the margin, the developing country preferring to produce domestically some would-be imports instead of obtaining them through exports. If that country wished to obtain certain goods that cannot be produced domestically, however, it would push ahead with exports of manufactures, if not of primary commodities, in spite of worsened terms of trade, and imports would be reduced only through the impact of the worsened terms of trade on income (and savings) affecting the need for input imports. However, according to the alternative theory suggested here, foreign obstacles to imports from developing countries will lead to a deterioration in their terms of trade and, in this way, reduce the factor rewards in certain sectors below the critical minimum level. In this way, balance-of-payments difficulties *could* be ascribed to obstacles applied by the advanced countries to the exports of developing countries.

Let us now look at the possibility that the foreign-exchange problems of developing countries are the result of overspending. It has already been pointed out several times that the foreign-exchange-gap analysis does not rule out the possibility that many developing countries compound their balance-of-payments problems through inept expenditure policies. Indeed, there would be no difficulty in finding economists prepared to argue that the actual balance-of-payments difficulties are *solely* the result of bad monetary and fiscal policies. For instance, in the so-called Haberler report, commissioned by the General Agreement on Tariffs and Trade (GATT), it is stated that "in order to increase the quantity of capital goods at the disposal of non-industrial countries, two things can be done: firstly, capital can be transferred from industrial to non-industrial countries; and secondly, the latter countries may step up their savings."[29] However, the way in which increased domestic savings are transformed into actual investments is not indicated. It is simply pointed out that "any forthcoming domestic savings should, of course, be invested in such a manner as to further in the best possible way the growth of the country's productive capacity."[30] This simple treatment should be expected as long as conventional theory is applied, but it is, nonetheless, surprising, because, not more than half a page further on, the same report goes on to observe that "roughly speaking, this item [imports of capital goods] tends to be proportional to gross investment in the economies concerned. A relatively modest speeding up of development will considerably raise the import requirements of capital goods. An 'acceleration principle' of a kind is at work."[31]

This statement amounts to nothing less than a recognition of the existence of a factor-proportions problem, i.e., of the existence of, at least, an import minimum. But if the increased domestic savings cannot be transformed into capital goods through domestic production, they can be transformed only through trade. One would thus expect the report to contain a careful statement of how increased savings would necessarily result in exports of such volume that there is no need to bother about the implications of an export maximum. But the brief section on the prospects for export earnings centers on the future demand for primary commodities in advanced countries, something that has very little to do with exports as a function of the rate of savings in developing countries. It would seem as if, as in the foreign-exchange-gap analysis, an increased propensity to save would rather increase the import need, in order to avoid frustration of the savings potential, than increase the actual exports. The Haberler report, although basing its analysis on conventional theory, thus hardly substantiates the applicability of this theory to the trade problem of developing countries, but rather arrives at the central problem through a self-contradiction. As might be expected, it is not difficult to find many other instances where the prevailing theory has been applied to underdeveloped countries, and the balance-of-payments strains of these countries explained in terms of inept expenditure policies.[32] The discussion in the Haberler report should be a sufficient example.

Even within the analytical framework suggested here, however, the actual balance-of-payments deficits *could* be the result of conventional overspending and thus need not be a sign of acute foreign-exchange gaps. To substantiate the hypothesis that there exist foreign-exchange gaps as defined here, an analysis of the balance of payments must go beyond the net positions on the accounting balance of payments. This is true for the additional reason that equilibrium on the accounting balance of payments does not exclude the possibility of a deficit on the program balance, such an equilibrium having been achieved through measures incompatible with internal equilibrium.

To begin with, let us consider the question whether there is any overexpenditure in the developing countries

that reduces the supply of exportables. It seems highly
unlikely, at least with respect to primary products. The
volume of primary-product exports has increased, and
more rapidly than export proceeds. The commodity terms
of trade have been falling.[33] This suggests that the developing countries have been approaching the export maximum for this export category and that continued supply
increases beyond the trendwise demand increase (i.e., beyond shifts in the demand curve adjusting upward through
time the export maximum) will soon lead to lower export
receipts. The situation is more uncertain with manufactures. But the production structure in developing countries
is such that there can hardly be any important diversion
of potential exports to meet overbuoyant home demand.
The impression given by the statistics, that the export
maximum has been approached, rather than that the export opportunities have been ruined by inefficient expenditure policies, is strengthened by various analyses
of the export problems of underdeveloped countries, including developing countries and regions.[34] Typically,
these result in negative conclusions as to the possibilities
of expanding manufactured exports, owing to various
structural difficulties on the supply side, rather than to
exorbitant prices or internal demand pressures.

The extent to which the actual balance-of-payments
difficulties of developing countries are due to conventional
overspending on imports can, perhaps, be estimated
through a study of the composition of imports into developing countries. The share of "manufactured consumer
goods"—a category reported separately by GATT up to
1962—is low, amounting to some 17 per cent. Although a
definite classification of imports into input imports and
non-input imports cannot be made without a closer
analysis of the actual use of the various import items,[35] it
might be surmised that this commodity category approxi-
mates the total value of non-input imports. It is possible
that some of these goods would, on closer examination,
prove to be input imports; but this might be offset by some
other imports that would be found to be non-inputs, although not classified as "manufactured consumer goods."

In absolute terms, such imports amount to some U.S. $3.5 billion. Even if freeing this foreign exchange for other purposes would represent a substantial improvement, it is doubtful that imports of manufactured consumer goods could be significantly reduced through optimum expenditure policies. Virtually all developing countries already operate severe import restrictions, many of them through direct controls—and for the explicit purpose of improving their balance of payments. These measures, which are incompatible with conventional theory, must be expected to be as efficient as general expenditure policies in reducing imports of "inessentials."[36] Probably, the imports of "inessentials" that exist today cannot significantly be eliminated without negative repercussions on incentives and on Keynesian effective demand. Among underdeveloped countries, those with an important developing sector already have a below-average share of manufactured consumer-goods imports.

Thus, the structure of imports may indicate that the balance-of-payments pressures from the import side cannot be fully ascribed to inadequate expenditure policies and overimportation of non-inputs. This supposition is strengthened by the observations that foreign-exchange difficulties have, in fact, proved serious enough as to necessitate some curtailment in input imports, even for operation purposes. Such reductions mean an underutilization of existing physical production capacity; they have nonetheless proved unavoidable. For instance, Kitamura writes that "In the Asian region, we have to consider a typical underdeveloped economy whose rate of growth is . . . limited by the stagnating export-based capacity to import. Disequilibria, structural in the sense that underemployment and underutilization of domestic resources are combined with external deficits, are one of the common features of the economies in the region."[37]

This passage indicates that the balance-of-payments problems do not merely reflect a lack of opportunities to import an unrealistic amount of expansion imports and thus to reach a romantically high rate of growth. This recieves additional documentation in the Indian Third Five

Year Plan. Commenting on the amount of foreign exchange set aside in the plan for maintenance imports,
the authors state that "Actually, the needs are larger. . . .
Nevertheless, it is not possible at this stage to provide
more resources for this purpose. This means that some
underutilization of capacity will have to be tolerated."[38]

According to Lakdawala, there are 237 industries for
which installed capacity figures were available for India in
1963.[39] Of these, only 130 were working at a capacity of
80 per cent or more, and as many as 49 at a capacity of
60 per cent or less. Full capacity has been calculated in
most of the industries on the basis of only one shift being
worked during only three hundred working days. These
figures are all the more depressing as the calculations
of installed capacity were made in 1962, and, in quite a
few cases, there had been substantial additions to capacity
up to the period when the production data were collected.
Lakdawala attributes the low level of capacity utilization
to the shortage of foreign exchange in particular.

In a forthcoming book, Waterston reports widespread
underutilization of capacity in underdeveloped countries
—the Philippines, Taiwan, Pakistan, and India—due to
foreign-exchange difficulties. As his own conclusion, he
quotes from Economic Commission for Asia and the
Far East (ECAFE): " 'The question is whether fuller utilization of existing plants should not be given priority
over installation of new industrial undertakings.' "[40] Sid-
ney Dell of the U.N. Economic Secretariat has also underlined the fact that underutilization of existing resources
is a common feature of the developing countries: "One of
the paradoxes about underdeveloped countries is that,
while they obviously need many more factories and industries, they do not fully utilize the industrial capacity
they already have."[41] He complains that, although this
fact is well attested, it is not easy to document as fully
as one would wish. (He quotes, however, certain data from
Chile and Mexico.)

To the extent that there has been a curtailment of
maintenance imports, it would be plausible to expect
that expansion imports have had to be reduced on an even

greater scale. This is likely since, after all, there should be little interest in expanding a production apparatus that cannot be fully used.[42] It would, of course, be difficult to prove this because the category "frustrated savings" is singularly elusive. However, it may, in this situation, be illuminating to look at some statistics regarding capital formation and gross national products.

In Table 2, an attempt is made to calculate *for illustrative purposes* the amount of savings that were frustrated during the periods 1953-60 in Latin America. By dividing savings data (column 4)—calculated by adding the current-account balance to investment data—by GNP (column 2), the *ex-post* propensity to save is obtained (column 5). As variations in investment can be assumed to be a function of variations in imports, it can be argued that any changes in the *ex-post* propensity to save are due to changes in the availability of imports. Taking the highest observed propensity to save during the period in question (0.173), and assuming no lack of input imports in that particular year, so that no savings were frustrated, this propensity may be used to calculate the amount of frustrated savings during the other years. In column 6, GNP has been multiplied by this *ex-ante* propensity to save (0.173) to obtain planned savings. In column 7, realized savings in each year have been deducted from planned savings. The sum total gives the total amount of savings frustrated during the period—$8 billion. If the highest observed propensity to save had not been equal to the *ex-ante* propensity to save, these results would, of course, have had to be adjusted upward. Similarly, if the compounded effect of frustrated savings on GNP had been taken into account, the sum would have been higher. But it is unnecessary to go into any complications, because the method as such is clearly open to criticism and is, it should be repeated, suggested purely for illustrative purposes.

There is another interesting way in which it may be possible to find support for the concepts of export maxima and import minima which, in fact, create foreign-exchange gaps as defined here: the projections of import needs

TABLE 2

Attempted Estimate of Frustrated Savings in Latin America

1	2	3	4	5	6	7
Year	GNP (Billions of U.S. Dollars)	I (Billions of U.S. Dollars)	S	s	S_p ($s_p = 0.173$) (Billions of U.S. Dollars)	$S_p - S$ (Billions of U.S. Dollars)
1953	43.8	7.4	7.6	0.173	7.6	–
1954	47.0	8.4	7.9	0.168	8.1	0.2
1955	49.4	8.8	8.2	0.166	8.5	0.3
1956	51.1	9.0	8.3	0.162	8.8	0.5
1957	54.9	9.5	7.2	0.135	9.5	2.3
1958	56.8	9.7	8.1	0.143	9.8	1.7
1959	58.3	9.5	8.8	0.151	10.1	1.7
1960	61.4	10.1	9.3	0.151	10.6	1.3
Total						8.0

Sources: GNP and capital-formation data from United Nations, *World Economic Survey, 1963* (New York, 1964), Part I, (New York, 1964), Table 3 A-2, p. 37; current-account figures ($S - I$) from *World Economic Survey, 1963,* Part I, p. 255 and from United Nations, *Statistical Yearbook, 1963,* (New York, 1964), pp. 450-51. Dollar values are in 1960 prices and exchange rates.

Method of construction: Total savings (S) are calculated by adding the balance on current-account to investments (I), the propensity to save (s) is calculated by dividing total savings (S) by GNP; *ex-ante* savings (S_p) are calculated by equating the *ex-ante* propensity to save with 0.173, i.e., the highest value for s during the period in question, assuming that in that year (1953) all *ex-ante* savings could be realized and that the *ex-ante* propensity to save would not have changed through time. By deducting actual savings from planned savings ($S_p - S$), the total amount of frustrated savings during the period (U.S. $8.0 billion) is obtained.

and export potential of underdeveloped countries over a
number of years. Such projections have, for instance,
been made in the U.N. and the GATT secretariats and by
Bela Balassa. Although these projections are for all
underdeveloped countries, the chief characteristics of the
results must be determined by the situation of the developing countries and regions.

All three projections point to a gap between need and
availability. In the discussion of palliatives, there is no
mention of the central balancing mechanism, a cut in domestic expenditure. The approach, therefore, implies a
break with traditional theory, and the gap that is calculated
must be identical to the foreign-exchange gap defined in
this study.

The U.N. study was made for the U.N. Conference on
Trade and Development—in itself a manifestation of the
concern over the foreign-exchange problems arising in
connection with development—and is published in *World
Economic Survey, 1962,* Part I.[43] Three different deficits
on the program balance of payments for 1970 are arrived
at—$20 billion, $11 billion, and $4 billion. The first
deficit is on current account; the second deficit emerges
when a calculated inflow of capital and donations has
been taken into account; the third deficit is the gap that
remains after a number of policy actions are assumed
to have been implemented. Regarding this last, the policy
actions are, interestingly enough, not assumed to include
a conventional cut in expenditures, which, according to
conventional theory, should bring about external balance and internal balance simultaneously. None of the
three gaps corresponds exactly to the foreign-exchange
gap as defined in the present study. A foreign-exchange
gap would be equal to the gap between autonomous items
in the program balance of payments, assuming conventional trade policies and optimum expenditure policies
and, to avoid a frustration of the domestic growth potential, assuming that the programed foreign-exchange
requirements do not exceed the needs. However, the first
of the U.N. gaps excludes some autonomous items, and
the second and third includes some accommodating items.

Furthermore, it is not quite clear whether the foreign-exchange requirements are based on what would be needed to attain a socially acceptable rate of growth, rather than on what would be needed to avoid a frustration of resource additions. Another difference is that the projections are made on the assumption that there will be continued severe trade restrictions on non-input imports. They are, in addition, based on data for the 1950's, when actual imports were probably smaller than the import minimum, i.e., when an internal imbalance had been substituted for a part of the external disequilibrium. However, even if the U.N. measurements do not fully concur with the concepts used in the foreign-exchange-gap analysis, it is interesting to note that the basic approach involves an estimate of what, to all intents and purposes, amounts to acute foreign-exchange gaps.

The GATT study is contained in *International Trade, 1961*.[44] There is no need to go through the calculations in detail. It will suffice to note that a sizable deficit, estimated at $5–15 billion, is again projected between "minimal import requirements" and "traditional exports." Furthermore, among the methods mentioned to bridge the gulf, there is no reference to a conventional cut in expenditures.

The Balassa projection, finally, perhaps the most carefully made of the three,[45] also reaches the conclusion that in 1970 there will be a program deficit on current account of some U.S. $5 billion, although it criticizes the other two studies for overestimating future program balance-of-payments deficits, mainly through overestimating future import needs.

In trying to substantiate the foreign-exchange-gap analysis, it has been difficult to illustrate empirically the existence of an export maximum and to show that developing countries are close to this maximum. From that point of view, it is particularly interesting to note how, negatively, the possibilities of increasing exports are ascertained. Balassa, for instance, estimates that from 1960 to 1970 manufactured exports (other than metals) to advanced countries will increase from U.S.

$1.1 billion to U.S. $1.8 billion and that the percentage of such exports in the total of exports from developing country to advanced countries will remain low.[46]

There are, then, a number of studies projecting a deficit on the program balance of payments of developing countries, in terms that must be understood to mean that a conventional cut in expenditures can only lead to internal disequilibrium. It would, in fact, be rather odd to calculate the size of such deficits, if they do not imply the existence of foreign-exchange gaps as defined in this study, but could be closed through the use of conventional balance-of-payments equilibrators.

The approach to the balance-of-payments problems of developing countries underlying this kind of projection originates from the writings of a number of economists, especially economists from the underdeveloped countries themselves. Apart from Kitamura and S. J. Patel, already quoted, the economists most representative in this context include W. A. Lewis, I. G. Patel, R. Prebisch, and V. L. Urquidi.[47] The following quotation from Patel illustrates well the basic and characteristic argument for this group:

> Economic growth sets up demands for imports which are too large for the small export sector to meet, especially when this export sector is confined to a range of goods for which world demand is not particularly responsive. To put it differently, internal resources cannot always be converted into the required machines or materials or consumer goods in adequate quantities either directly by internal production or indirectly by providing large enough export receipts. The balance of payments barrier, ... generally appears before the inflation barrier so that the balance of payments difficulties of developing countries are not necessarily a reflection of inadequate savings or of inflationary fiscal and monetary policies. This is not to say that inadequate savings are not a factor in the situation or that many if not most cases of balance of payments difficulties are not generally aggravated by inflationary policies. Nor does it deny that there are obvious cases among the less developed countries where even a single export product can earn more than sufficient

foreign exchange to sustain all the development that is otherwise possible. Nevertheless, as a general rule, the less
developed countries suffer from such a limited degree of
manoeuvrability in their balance of payments that it is
meaningful to refer to their balance of payments problems
as something distinct from a mere manifestation of inadequate savings or inappropriate fiscal and monetary policies.[48]

It is by no means only economists from underdeveloped countries, however, who have expressed views that
run counter to accepted trade doctrine, but harmonize
well with the approach here. For instance, Hirschman
has argued that it is at least conceivable that the balance-of-payments difficulties of particular underdeveloped countries appear directly, "as a result of some
typical growth sequences, rather than exclusively as a
reflection of domestic inflation."[49]

In order to develop this idea, Hirschman assumes that
we divide a developing economy in two parts: an R-sector,
which can grow rapidly, and an S-sector, which can only
grow slowly. If the output of the S-sector must be used
as inputs in the R-sector, the growth rate of the R-sector
in the absence of trade cannot be higher than that of the
S-sector. If there is an opportunity to trade, it might be
stepped up, through imports of inputs that are not produced in a sufficient quantity in the domestic S-sector,
but depends on the "exportability" of the products produced by the R-sector. This "exportability" is, Hirschman says, low for most presently developing countries.
The similarity of approach is evident. Conditions in the
R-sector, although not specified by Hirschman, set an
export maximum and the impotence of the S-sector means
an import minimum, with the possibility of an acute
foreign-exchange gap being emphasized. Finally, Hirschman concludes, as we have done, that the industrializing
latecomers have a need "less for 'a supplement of real
resources' than for some *specific additional imports, no
matter whether they are obtained by trade or by aid.*[50]

During the last few years, a number of economists who
are not from underdeveloped countries have made con-

tributions which are even more reminiscent than Hirschman's model of the analytical framework suggested here. They accept the various projections of a foreign-exchange gap for underdeveloped countries and discuss the role of trade and of foreign aid in terms of a "foreign exchange constraint" on development. This constraint is assumed to exist along with a savings constraint and a skill and management constraint. Its implications have then been explored. However, it is never demonstrated in these writings how, considering the analysis of existing trade theory, a foreign-exchange constraint could prevail without simply being the reflection of insufficient domestic savings or inept expenditure policies. To show this would seem to be the crucial task, both in order to establish the new approach and in order to evaluate the continued usefulness of conventional doctrine. Yet these contributions, like the others that have been surveyed here, point to a spreading dissatisfaction with existing trade theory and a widening belief that trade has a more crucial role but also a less easily attained role than could be expected on the basis of current doctrine. A typical example of this attitude is the calculations by Manne of the sizable increases in production that could be realized in Mexico with a minor additional input of foreign exchange.[51]

It is obvious that various more or less telling pieces of empirical evidence, as well as the thinking of a substantial number of economists, can be accommodated in the foreign-exchange-gap analysis, rather than in conventional theory. This is, of course, not sufficient to prove that the theory of trade and developing countries presented here is widely applicable but it does mean that it is sufficiently so to call for a systematic exploration of its policy conclusions—a task that will be undertaken in the next chapter of this study. Even if this theory had no applicability, it would nonetheless have a *raison d'être* in that it provides a systematic investigation of the conditions under which a theory of import minima and export maxima *would be* applicable. This is important, for the essentials of such a theory do seem, in fact, to be applied, at least implicitly, in the developing countries themselves.

TRADE AMONG DEVELOPING COUNTRIES AND TRADE
  WITH BACKWARD COUNTRIES

The import minimum–export maximum analysis of
trade with advanced countries cannot be applied to trade
with other developing countries, or trade with backward
countries. Apart from any primary inputs that may be
imported from other developing countries and from backward countries, there is no tight limitation on the substitutability between domestic factors and imported
inputs. Furthermore, the limits we observed on exports
to advanced countries are not applicable here, as the
demand structures of importer and exporter are much
more similar. Given appropriate expenditure policies,
therefore, it should be possible to achieve external balance
in trade with these countries without creating internal
disequilibrium, or without aggravating the disequilibrium
that may have resulted from inability to cover a foreign-
exchange gap arising in trade with advanced countries.

If balance in these trade flows need not preclude internal equilibrium, then the neoclassical allocation analysis would be applicable to the intratrade of developing
countries and to their trade with backward countries. This
trade would enable the developing countries to achieve a
superior allocation of those resources that, depending
upon the amount of operation imports coming from advanced countries, happen to be employed. It would also
bring the additional benefits of economies of scale and
increased competition, all in accordance with conventional
theory.

As expounded in the survey of conventional trade
theory, trade would also have certain growth implications by providing a necessary condition (static efficiency)
for dynamic efficiency. However, it is questionable whether
this growth effect will be of any consequence in the case
of trade with other developing countries or backward countries. If there is an acute foreign-exchange gap, the
accumulation of additional resources cannot be stimu-

lated, as there is an M_i/m constraint that has already prevented the full realization of a smaller volume of planned savings. The provision of static efficiency would thus only appear to make a potential growth-engine even more potential. However, the implications of this important difference from conventional theory may be limited by some other, still more important, differences.

Trade with other developing countries and with backward countries is likely to reduce the need for operation imports from advanced countries. This is so because various primary commodities can be secured from countries other than the advanced ones. It is also possible that trade, at least with other developing countries, can lead to a certain reduction in the range of those non-inputs which might be imported under conventional commercial policies. A reduced need for operation imports from advanced countries (a reduction in the fraction p) means two things: (1) if the foreign-exchange gap was initially so severe that there was underutilization of existing capacity, there can be an increase in capacity utilization; and (2) foreign exchange can be freed from operation imports and used for investment imports (i.e., M_i will be increased) with no frustration, or reduced frustration, of savings as a result. Any reduction in non-input imports would free exchange for input imports, i.e., increase M_o and/or M_i.

Through a reduction in the fraction p and increase in M_o, this kind of trade will lead to an increase in capacity use, if there has been any underutilization to begin with. An increase in M_i will increase growth. It must be noted, however, that the provision of static efficiency will increase the savings potential, too. The increase in M_i might or might not enable the savings potential to be fully utilized. However, even if the volume of planned savings increases more than the amount of investment imports, so that the foreign-exchange gap would actually be widened, growth will increase as long as there is some increase in investment imports.

Of course, there are a number of other factors that tend to reduce the direct applicability of the neoclassical theory to trade with other developing and with backward countries. Among these, the lack of competition (not only within developing *countries* but even within the developing *sectors* of these countries) ranks high. These and other imperfections will lead to marginal inequalities and complications in the form of second-best considerations. But these factors can be handled, at least formally, in the neoclassical theory. They need not detract, therefore, from its applicability, except in the sense that its most simplified and well-known version would be open to considerable criticism.

Conventional theory may thus be used to give a reasonable approximation of the effects of trade between developing countries and with backward countries, even if certain modifications must be made in the underlying assumptions. It is thus important that the criticism of neoclassical theory as being inapplicable to developing countries is not carried too far and generalized to rule out its use in clarifying the effects of such trade flows.

Finally, although conventional trade theory helps in the analysis of the effects on *developing* countries of trade with backward countries, it is not necessarily so helpful with respect to the effects of such trade on the *backward* countries. This is analogous to the fact that effects of trade with developing countries on *advanced* countries can be analyzed with the help of conventional theory, whereas the analysis of the effects of such trade on *developing* countries calls, as we know, for a special theory. (The effects on backward countries of trade with advanced, developing, and other backward countries will be discussed in more detail in chapter 4.) This concluding observation means that, in countries with dual economies, the analysis of domestic trade requires the use of two different trade theories.

III

A Trade Policy for
Developing Countries

Under the most simple set of conventional assumptions, free trade is the policy through which it is possible to maximize world income. Free trade has this effect through optimizing the allocation of existing resources. In this way, it also provides a necessary condition for dynamic efficiency. Free trade would thus be the best policy to maximize both present and future income.

Some of the assumptions underlying the case for free trade, however, have been relaxed as part of neoclassical analysis, and the free-trade doctrine has been subjected to certain well-known qualifications.

1. The proposition that free trade is better than restricted trade applies only if it is *world* income that is to be maximized. If the income of a particular country is to be maximized, this country could probably gain by levying certain tariffs to improve its terms of trade. The losses from misallocation which the country would have to sustain from such "optimum tariffs" would be more than offset by better terms of trade, but at the expense of world welfare. The national gains from an optimum tariff would probably, but not necessarily, be turned into losses, should other countries retaliate.[1] As to the growth implications of optimum tariffs, it is, as usual, possible to argue that if the particular country has the highest income it can possibly attain, then it also has the best basis for growth. However, since world income is negatively affected, the growth rate for the world as a whole is likely to be reduced. Here the outcome will also depend upon international differences in savings propensities.[2]

2. Free competition may not be attained. If it is assumed that deficiencies exist in the pricing mechanism of a country and that thus, in even more technical language, standard "first-best" conditions do not prevail, different conclusions follow. It *might* then be advantageous for the country in question to institute certain tariffs in order to reach an optimum resource allocation for national—and world—welfare-maximization purposes. One type of distortion is that emphasized in the Manoilesco case for protection, i.e., where wages in manufacturing are higher than in agriculture. Measures correctly applied to counteract distortions could be assumed to provide the best basis for growth, too.[3]

3. Tariffs might be needed to take advantage of external economies. The most important instance of such tariffs would be infant-industry protection.[4] The *rationale* of this tariff argument is that, although the tariffs in question would mean inferior allocation in the economy in the short run, they could increase the return on existing resources in the long run and might increase the rate of accumulation of additional resources by providing a better investment climate.

These three arguments for tariffs are the ones that are "economically respectable" in conventional theory. A number of protectionist arguments are "semirespectable" from an economic point of view, e.g., tariffs for revenue purposes and protection to increase foreign investment ("tariff factories"). Protection for military purposes might be acceptable on political grounds. But there are two important arguments that are not acceptable in conventional theory: protection for balance-of-payments purposes, and protection to increase effective demand for domestic products in order to eliminate underemployment ("beggar-my-neighbor policies"); i.e., protection to cure external disequilibrium and internal disequilibrium, respectively.[5] These two protectionist arguments are rejected on basically the same grounds, i.e., that external and internal equilibrium can be established through appropriate expenditure policies and that trade policy should then be used to optimize the allocation of resources. It is, for instance, better to cure an external deficit by making a general reduction and shift in expenditure and trading according to comparative advantages than by producing domestically goods in which the country has a comparative disadvantage. More resources would be used up in this domestic production than in the production of exportable products to pay for the imports, whether or not the latter were "luxury" goods.[6] Similarly, it would be better to cure internal underemployment through a general increase and shift in expenditure, so as to increase effective demand without damaging the allocative efficiency. These arguments do not preclude an analysis in a Keynesian context of the possibilities of increasing effective demand through a shift in expenditure away from imports by means of controls.

Restrictions on trade imposed for either of these two reasons are sometimes defended by the argument that their removal would lower the income of the country through terms-of-trade losses more than it would increase income through improved allocative efficiency of the economy. But this is nothing more than the optimum-tariff argument, applied to defend a policy the original motive for which was different. It seems appropriate analytically to keep the two arguments apart. Assuming that a country levies an optimum tariff as part of a perfect trade policy, there can never be a separate case for any restrictions for balance-of-payments or business-cycle purposes. In conventional trade theory, therefore, there is a case for the maintenance of restrictions to cure internal or external disequilibrium only when this case collapses into the case for optimum tariffs.

The importance attributed to the recognized qualifications to the free-trade doctrine varies. It is probably fair to conclude that, in practice, the amendments, with the possible exception of the infant-industry argument, are regarded as theoretical refinements rather than as

suggestions for practical policy. The reason for this is
to be found in the great analytical, administrative, and
political difficulties, or costs, of formulating—and re-
formulating as circumstances change—and operating the
particular set of trade restrictions that could be sanc-
tioned in theory. And it must be remembered that, just
because restricted trade may be found to be better than
free trade, *any* set of restrictions is not better than free
trade. The costs of finding the appropriate set of restrictions and of changing it through time may well be
prohibitive. One should not try to be "rational" if the
cost of finding the rational solution is greater than the
gains. On the basis of conventional theory, most theorists would probably agree that the costs of protection
will, in practice, exceed the gains. Free trade may thus
be regarded as the recommended *practical policy*.[7]

When the commercial-policy doctrine derived from
the conventional theory of international trade has been
applied to underdeveloped countries, the protectionist
arguments have appeared stronger. The optimum-tariff
case is strengthened, on account of the low elasticity of
demand for imports of primary commodities in advanced
countries. The pricing mechanism in underdeveloped
countries must be expected to work very inefficiently;
therefore, measures like the Manoilesco-Hagen corrective tariffs become more relevant. Finally, a case for
infant-industry protection may not exist at all other than
in underdeveloped countries.

However, the arguments *against* protection are also
strengthened. These arguments take the form of a re-
minder of the administrative costs of formulating an appropriate set of trade obstacles. These costs could be
considerable, for it is difficult to avoid worsening, rather
than improving, the allocative ability when one tries to
offset deficiencies in the price mechanism. Similarly,
when optimum tariffs are devised, allocation could be
damaged more than the terms of trade are improved.

The conclusion must be that there is scope for much
disagreement in conventional theory on what the optimum

trade policy for underdeveloped countries should be. In fact, there certainly is great disagreement. On the one hand, it seems as if many theoretical economists have concluded that, on balance, free trade is still to be regarded as the most recommendable policy. Harberger, for instance, has tried to calculate for Chile how much the GNP would increase if all tariffs—assuming a general tariff level of 50 per cent to begin with—were removed. He concludes that the flow of factors of production out of the relatively inefficient lines of activity into more competitive pursuits would increase the GNP by some 2.5 per cent.[8] On the other hand, as noted in the introductory chapter, there is no difficulty in finding authors who advocate, within the confines of conventional theory, the application of protectionist measures.

Actual commercial policies in developing countries are far removed from free trade. High tariffs, extensive quantitative restrictions, and far-reaching exchange regulations are the rule rather than the exception. This could be interpreted as evidence that policy-makers have been impressed more by those advocating protectionist measures within the framework of conventional theory than by those opposing such measures in practical grounds. But many economists, especially from underdeveloped countries, have rejected conventional theory as being generally inapplicable to developing countries. It would therefore seem more plausible to argue that actual policies reflect, instead, a totally different view of the role of trade. The conflict over commercial policies in developing countries is probably not so much a conflict between different evaluations of the relevance of the protectionist arguments in the traditional theory as a conflict between the traditional theory and a wholly different approach. In any case, the policies do not reflect a well-defined set of conclusions derived from a neat body of theory, but represent an intuitive rejection of existing theory and a search for alternative policies based on rather fragmentary theories of trade. As is so often the case, actual policies seem to precede explicit theories from which these policies could be deduced.

Trade Policy Vis-à-Vis Advanced Countries

As most developing countries are typically exposed to substantial instability with respect to foreign payments and receipts, and since it is impractical for such countries to change the nature of their commercial policy frequently, the policy principles set out here apply to all countries that may, potentially or actually, face foreign-exchange gaps. (On the basis of empirical evidence, it could be surmised that this includes all developing countries except, *as yet*, some countries like Kuwait and Bahrein.[9]) The existence of a foreign-exchange gap means that the basic postulate of conventional commercial policy, simultaneous internal and external equilibrium, cannot be upheld. This suggests that there must be a reformulation, rather than a modification, of the theory of conventional commercial policy.

To illustrate the situation, it may be convenient to have recourse to a diagram in terms of demand and supply curves of foreign exchange. On the vertical axis in Figure 4, the rate of exchange (the price of one unit of foreign currency in terms of the developing country's currency) is measured. An upward movement along the axis means a devaluation of the developing country's currency because more has to be paid for one unit of foreign currency; a downward movement implies an appreciation, until at the origin, the price of the foreign currency is zero. The horizontal axis measures the quantity of foreign exchange.

In order to bring out the task of commercial policy, the curves illustrate the demand and supply situation, under the assumption that internal balance is being preserved and a conventional trade policy is being pursued. The foreign-exchange gap now emerges clearly in the diagram. The supply curve, representing earnings on

Figure 4

Exchange Rate
(cost of one unit of foreign
exchange in terms of domestic currency)

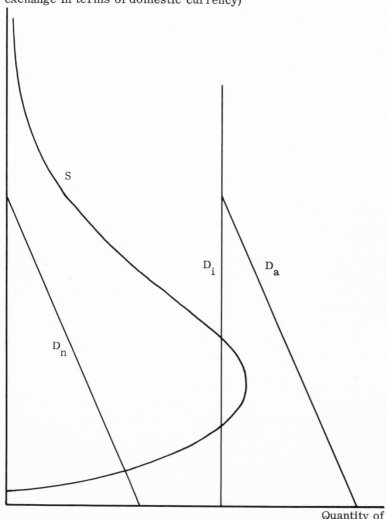

S

D_i

D_a

D_n

Quantity of
Foreign Exchange

current account, shows the general properties of supply curves of foreign exchange.[10] The demand curve, however, differs from ordinary demand curves of foreign exchange. Demand for foreign exchange is composed of two elements, exchange to pay for input imports and exchange to pay for non-input imports. The demand curve for the latter (D_n) shows the general characteristics of demand curves for foreign exchange. It intercepts the y-axis at some high price of foreign exchange and has a negative slope down to a finite quantity of foreign exchange when the price of foreign exchange is zero.[11] Demand for input imports, and thus demand for foreign exchange to pay for them, is, however, assumed to amount to what is needed to avoid internal disequilibrium. The demand curve for foreign exchange to pay for input imports (D_i) is thus *ex definitione* completely inelastic.[12] The aggregate demand curve (D_a) can therefore be drawn as being kinked. The kink appears at that exchange rate where the demand for foreign exchange to pay for non-inputs becomes zero. *The aggregate demand curve does not intersect the supply curve.* This is the distinguishing feature of the foreign-exchange situation of a country exposed to a foreign-exchange gap.

Our task is now to design a trade policy that would enable a country to alleviate the negative effects of a foreign-exchange gap and avoid closing the foreign-exchange gap through an enforced leftward movement of the D_i curve, i.e., through substituting internal imbalance for external. Figure 4 suggests three principle ways in which a solution to this problem could be found: (1) measures designed to move the aggregate demand curve for foreign exchange farther to the left without cutting back the required quantity of input imports; (2) measures designed to move the supply curve for foreign exchange farther out to the right; and (3) measures designed to bridge the foreign-exchange gap through capital-account transactions.

As might be expected, some of the measures that fall under these three headings amount to recommendations to deviate, if certain conditions can be fulfilled, from the doctrine that the role of trade is to optimize the allocation of resources (whether this, in practice, has meant free trade or some system of tariffs).

However, even if an interventionist trade policy may be required to secure certain capacity and growth gains, would it not, at the same time, cause allocation losses as set out in conventional theory? Is there not a conflict between the aim to achieve optimum allocation, on the one hand, and higher capacity use and a quicker pace of capacity growth, on the other? This is a most important question, which must be answered before anything definite can be said about the trade policy for countries facing a foreign-exchange gap.

There is no such conflict in conventional trade theory, because an improvement in capacity and the balance of payments which could be secured through protection could also be achieved through appropriate expenditure policies —and then without the allocation losses that would result from protection. The case is thus unequivocally for using trade policy to optimize allocation. But in the analytical framework suggested here, the capacity gains cannot be secured through appropriate expenditure policies. Such gains must therefore be attributed to commercial-policy measures, and, *if* there are simultaneous allocation losses from these measures, there will exist an indeterminate situation from a policy point of view.

This kind of conflict will not arise, however, because there will, in fact, be no allocation losses to be deducted from the capacity gains. As long as the foreign-exchange gap remains open, there will be underutilization of domestic capacity, and the social cost of domestic factors will be zero. Thus, deviations from the allocation considerations of conventional theory do not mean that factors are taken from a more productive to a less productive activity. Therefore, the situation is the opposite to that in conventional theory. There, protection would lead to allocation losses without creating any other gains that could not be secured in some other way; here, protection would not lead to allocation losses but would yield capacity gains that cannot be achieved in any other fashion.

The argument that allocation considerations are of little significance, as the social cost of factors of production brought into employment through protection is zero, is not just a variant of the Manoilesco argument for protection. It is true that if social costs are zero, private costs are likely to be higher, so that there is a marginal inequality that may call for protection. However, the Manoilesco tariff would be levied to improve allocation in order to allow the doctrine of comparative advantage to be correctly applied. The protection suggested here would be imposed to increase capacity use and growth when the full advantages of trade could otherwise not be secured, the doctrine of comparative advantage being inoperative. The zero social costs are important only to demonstrate that there will be no reallocation losses. In fact, a divergence between social and private costs is not a necessary condition for the applicability of protection for capacity purposes. Even if private costs also happened to be zero, and there were no Manoilesco case for tariffs, protection to yield capacity gains could be necessary.

The proposition that there will be no reallocation losses when the marginal social costs are zero needs one important qualification, however. There is, as has already been emphasized, a risk that domestic factors will be allocated into uses where their value added proves to be *negative*, that they will be directed into something less productive than their present idleness. A negative value added means that factors are allocated into activities where their productivity is so low that imported inputs may be wasted. In the case of import substitution, this implies that the foreign-exchange cost of importing the final goods would be lower than that of importing the inputs required to produce the substitutes. And the value of the exports would be smaller than the value of the input imports used to produce them. It is interesting, in this context, to refer to various instances, reported by

Pryor, where attempts at import substitution in East European countries resulted in negative value added.[13] If this can befall the relatively advanced East European countries, it must be a serious risk for developing countries.

The important conclusion to be drawn from this is that there is an *efficiency criterion* that must be applied to trade-policy measures intended to yield capacity gains. If it is not met, the activity in question does not add to capacity or capacity use under any economically acceptable definition; furthermore, since it will necessitate the diversion of foreign exchange away from other uses, it will actually result in capacity losses. Thus, losses could be referred to, equally well, as capacity losses or as allocation losses. This is important in that it substantiates the proposition that there is no conflict between capacity and allocation considerations.

Finally, it should be noted that only so long as a foreign-exchange gap exists is there no conflict between allocation and capacity considerations. If it is possible to bridge the gap with the help of measures that, according to conventional theory, would not affect allocation negatively, these measures should be preferred. Among such measures may be mentioned the removal of foreign import restrictions and a stimulation of capital imports (except for capital imports that lead to servicing problems, to be discussed later).[14]

Measures to Reduce Foreign-Exchange Expenditure on Non-input Imports

As was observed in Chapter 2, a foreign-exchange gap can exist even if all imports are input imports. But it is likely that there will be certain non-input imports under a system of conventional trade policies, even if optimum expenditure policies are pursued.

One task for policy-makers in a developing country thus must be to explore the possibilities of reserving a maximum amount of the foreign-exchange earnings

for input imports. This means that non-input imports
must be cut back and that there is a case for trade restrictions.[15] Such measures may be required in order to
cure external disequilibrium without creating underutilization of domestic capacity, or—what is the same
thing looked at from the other direction—to cure internal
disequilibrium without upsetting the balance of payments.
Therefore, protection for balance-of-payments reasons
and for antidepression purposes obviously cannot be ruled
out. It may thus seem as if the two major protectionist
arguments that are not admitted in conventional theory
can be accepted here. Furthermore, since non-input imports may be considered "luxury imports," it is possible to recognize not only a general case for trade restrictions but also a particular method of selecting the
commodities to be restricted—a method that, although
often advocated, conflicts with conventional theory. However, although the *aims* of protection may look the same
in the two theories, the workings of protection in the two
cases widely differ.

Conventionally, protection to cure domestic overcapacity aims at increasing the effective demand for
domestic products—either at home, by reducing total
imports, or abroad, by stimulating exports. With the
existence of a foreign-exchange gap, however, protection
is advocated to increase the scope for a particular kind of
import—i.e., input imports. Or else, protection to improve
a balance-of-payments deficit is conventionally said to
produce a general reduction in imports; whereas, within
the alternative framework presented here, protection
would serve the purpose of avoiding the cutting back of
certain imports.

It should be pointed out that the difference in the process that is assumed to be started by protection in the
two approaches means that protection to cure a foreign-
exchange gap cannot be labeled as "beggar-my-neighbor"
policy. The purpose is not to increase effective demand
at the expense of foreign countries but to maximize imports of certain products within the scope of total im-

ports, the volume of which there is no wish to reduce. This difference is, perhaps, most clearly illustrated by the fact that a country pursuing "beggar-my-neighbor" policies might well be willing to pile up foreign-exchange reserves, whereas a developing country is rather in the opposite situation.

Import restrictions are easier to propose than to make effective, though. It is dangerous to subscribe to the "partial equilibrium" approach, i.e., to imagine that a declared curtailment of certain imports by a specific amount is synonymous with an improvement in the balance of payments or with increased scope for other imports by exactly the same sum of money.[16] Assume that a country imports passenger cars worth, say, $10 million and wants to free this foreign exchange for some other purpose. It therefore restricts the importation of passenger cars. A variety of things may now happen. The decisive factor is how the money that was formerly spent on passenger cars is now used. (1) The money may be spent on some other imported non-input, which is not subject to import controls. (2) It may be used to buy smuggled imports or for some other purpose that represents an evasion of the controls. (3) It may be spent on exportables or, at least, on goods produced by factors of production drawn from export activities. (4) It may be spent on import substitutes produced by formerly idle factors of production. (5) The money may be saved.[17] Any combination of these is also possible.

Of these five possibilities, the first three would lead to no improvement in the balance of payments. The last two, on the other hand, would lead to such an improvement. We must now investigate under what circumstances they can be realized.

The effect of import controls on savings is usually considered to be uncertain. Savings may increase *temporarily* (1) as a result of hesitation about how expenditures are to be reshuffled after the introduction or intensification of the controls, or (2) in anticipation of the removal of the controls, or (3) through disinvestment in inventories of imported non-input goods. But these temporary effects are rather unimportant, and the long-run effect may well, it has been argued, be negative. This would be the case if consumers, finding that their real income at an unchanged level of expenditure has decreased as a result of the import controls, cut down their savings in an effort to keep an unchanged level of satisfaction.[18] Moreover, it is sometimes added, even if there were a positive savings effect, this increase in savings would be more easily achieved through fiscal-policy measures.[19]

This analysis, which may or may not be accurate, is not applicable to developing countries, as must be obvious from the very fact that the trade controls are instituted in order to improve the balance of payments with the specific aim of preventing the *frustration of savings*. In the foreign-exchange-gap analysis, it is not indifferent, as it is in conventional theory, *which money* it is that is saved. As should be clear from the theoretical discussion, one cannot devote one's interest exclusively to *ex-post* savings without missing the essence of the whole argument. The crucial thing is *what happens to money spent on non-input imports*. If *that* money is saved, there can be an increase in input imports, which enables a realization of increased *ex-post* savings. If, on the other hand, there is an attempt to save money presently being spent on domestic goods, there will be no improvement in the balance of payments, no increase in input imports, and the attempt to save will fail—i.e., all that will happen is that the amount of frustrated savings will increase.

This argument also proves the erroneousness of the argument against trying to rely on a positive savings effect of import controls and in favor of using fiscal measures in general. For there *is* a chance of increasing, through controls, the possibility that money formerly spent on non-input imports will be saved. An attempt to increase savings through import controls may very well succeed, without this implying that optimum expenditure policies were not already being pursued. If there is an attempt to save the corresponding sum of money by means of the budget and there is no curtailment of non-input imports, there will only be an increase in frustrated savings, reduced incentives, and smaller domestic markets.

Still, attempts to use import controls to stimulate savings, although legitimate per se, are not certain to succeed. The principal way in which import controls could improve the balance of payments must, instead, be through the production of import substitutes. In this way, the expenditure on non-input imports need not be shifted into savings, but may be shifted into other goods, and will, nonetheless, improve the balance of payments.

Import substitution is often criticized as encouraging production of "inessential" goods. But if a country pursues optimal expenditure policies and there are still some imports of non-inputs, domestic production of these goods would not be "inessential," for it would enable the country to free more foreign exchange for input imports. It does not absorb factors that could be used elsewhere; it *enables* factors to be used elsewhere, both directly and indirectly, through the leverage effect of increased input imports.

It is not self-evident, however, that import substitution is a practical and practicable alternative. It is necessary to distinguish between whether import substitution is at all possible and whether it can be successful.

A necessary condition for import substitution is that there be unused capacity or frustrated additions to capacity in the economy. Otherwise, import controls must, if the savings alternative is disregarded, lead to any of the disadvantageous alternatives: increased imports of items not subject to controls, evasion of the controls,[20] consumption of the exportables, or, to the extent the goods formerly imported are now produced domestically, resources drawn from the production of exportables. If it is assumed that all non-input imports are controlled, there will thus be either a decrease in exports or evasion of the controls. It is impossible to tell a priori which of these two is the most important, since this will depend upon such factors as the efficiency of the administrative machinery and the relative cost of producing acceptable goods. It is probably true that the more developed a country is, the less controls are evaded and the greater the negative effects on export production. Both administrative considerations and relative production costs point in this direction.

Initial overcapacity (or threatening frustration of additions to capacity) being necessary for import substitution to save foreign exchange, it is interesting to note that developing countries have balance-of-payments problems *because of the very fact that there is an underutilization* of resources, which they have to try to cure by increasing input imports. Advanced countries usually have balance-of-payments problems *because there is overemployment* in the domestic economy. This is an important difference: the developing countries fulfill the necessary condition for foreign-exchange savings through import substitution; advanced nations are in practice unlikely to meet this condition—a fact that has not prevented balance-of-payments restrictions from being tried.

Developing countries thus, by definition, find themselves in the situation where a necessary condition for import substitution to save foreign exchange is fulfilled. But there is still no guarantee that the attempts at import substitution will successfully save foreign exchange. This is another important difference from the advanced countries, where, so long as the expenditure policies are assumed not to deteriorate, import substitution under conditions of initial overcapacity will succeed.[21]

There are two reasons why import substitution in developing countries may not be wholly successful in spite of persistent underutilization of capacity. First, there is the comparatively low productivity in the production of those goods that, in spite of optimum expenditure policies, are imported. Second, difficulties are encountered in financing the foreign-exchange component in the investments needed for the production of import-substitution goods.

As to the first problem, it is true that advanced countries also have relatively lower productivity with respect to those goods the importation of which they restrict so as to improve the balance of payments. It is for this reason that it would be better for them to improve their expenditure policies. For developing countries, however, the problem is not that costs are relatively high, but that, instead, the relative differences in productivity are likely to be so great that, although they ought to try to restrict imports, the success of the import substitution will be threatened.

First, productivity may be so low that domestic prices will be too high for the import substitutes to compete against smuggled imports. If, on the other hand, it is assumed that the administrative apparatus is efficient enough to hinder smuggling, there is a second way in which low productivity may thwart the success of import substitution: the production of the import substitutes may not meet the efficiency criterion.

For domestic factors not to have a negative value added, the value of input imports used in the production of import substitutes must not exceed the value of the imports to be substituted. The foreign-exchange cost of a particular project can be defined as expansion imports (M_e), plus the total value of operation imports used up during the lifetime of the project (tM_0), where t stands for the number of time periods making up the life of the investment. If the value of the imports replaced during the life of the investment is equal to P, the efficiency criterion may be written as

$$(M_e + tM_0) < P.$$

If both sides are divided by P, the criterion can be rewritten:

$$r < 1.$$

This criterion means that the fraction of expansion imports *plus* total operation imports (r) divided by replaced imports must be smaller than one. It is important to observe that P stands for the import cost that, in the absence of the import substitution, would be incurred in spite of optimum expenditure policies. Thus, it is not permissible to include in P the foreign-exchange value of domestically produced goods that do not replace would-be imports under optimum expenditure policies.

This criterion must be fulfilled for a project at the planning stage to be considered efficient. If the project has *already been realized*, the relevant criterion is less strict. It could then be written:

$$tM_O < P$$

or: $$p < 1,$$

i.e., the fraction of total operation imports divided by replaced imports must be lower than one, if continued production of the import substitutes during the life period of the initial investment is to save foreign exchange.[22] The foreign-exchange cost for the initial investment should be regarded as a sunk cost.

In stating the efficiency criteria thus, it is assumed that, for a particular import-substitution project to be considered efficient, it must be a net saver of foreign exchange over its lifetime. This may, however, be somewhat arbitrary, as the efficiency of the substitution is likely to *change through time*, for a number of reasons.

First, concurrently with the process of growth, import substitution is likely to occur spontaneously, i.e., even without protection. The "incremental comparative advantage," to use a concept coined by Nurkse,[23] probably lies with goods the demand for which becomes increasingly representative for the economy, but is not yet representative enough to permit fully competitive domestic production. Import substitution could thus be said to anticipate a future development, and, if efficient, will speed up this future development. What are the implications of this gradual increase? It means that the relevant time period within which import substitution must be a net saver of foreign exchange cannot, if the process is to be considered efficient, extend beyond the moment when full competitiveness would be achieved under all circumstances, whether or not this occurs during the lifetime of the first project.

Second, owing to the forces inherent in the learning period of the infant-industry argument, the efficiency is also likely to increase even if there is no particular growth effect on efficiency. The need for operation imports per unit of output is likely to fall. It is even possible that the lifetime of successive investments will increase, i.e., that investment imports per dollar of replaced imports will fall. This means that, although one particular project may be inefficient during its life period, it may be appropriate to go ahead with it in order to realize foreign-exchange savings during the life of subsequent projects of the same type.

The infant-industry case suggested here differs from the conventional infant-industry argument in some important respects.[24] The efficiency criterion itself differs in the two arguments. In the traditional case, it is required that the industry in question eventually prove efficient enough to offset the income losses suffered during the initial learning period.[25] In the infant-industry case for protection suggested here, it is, instead, required that the *foreign-exchange cost* on the input side of the project be more than offset on the output side. This efficiency criterion is weaker, as the project is not required to become internationally competitive, a difference in criteria that can exist because of the differences in the circumstances under which protection is applied. In the infant-industry case suggested here, the question is not one of gaining through a superior allocation of resources: it is one of instituting certain activities behind trade controls which, through foreign-exchange savings and increased input imports, enable the country to exert a leverage on capacity use and capacity growth. In contrast, the

conventional case holds even if all resources are fully
utilized, as the gains are derived from a reallocation.
Time (the learning period), but not growth, is essential to
the infant industry in the conventional argument, whereas
our case for protection is predicated on the overriding importance of the nonfrustration of resource accumulation.

The infant-industry case, as defined here, is thus of
much wider application than it tended to be in the neoclassical interpretation. In this context, it is interesting
to note that Myint, in a criticism of what he refers to as
"the traditional infant industry argument," concludes
that "the orthodox economists have, not surprisingly, reduced it to the status of a theoretical curiosity" by ex-
tracting "the protectionist argument from its original
context and applying it to minor derivations from the
static optimum. . . . It is only when the protectionist argument is reconsidered in its proper setting of the present-
day underdeveloped countries," Myint continues, "that
it can be restored to its full stature, having important applications to the broader structural and dynamic problems
of the economic development of these countries."[26]

The third and the most important consideration concerning the appropriate length of time on the basis of
which the efficiency of an import-substitution project
should be assessed, is of a somewhat different nature.
It is that *no import-substitution project can be efficient
during the very first stage*, i.e., during the investment
period. During the investment period, it necessarily uses
up foreign exchange without substituting any imports.

The importance of this observation is, of course, that,
even if an import-substitution project is efficient over
time, it may, owing to its *initial inefficiency*, be difficult
to realize the project when the very motive for its realization is a lack of foreign exchange. Although all eventually efficient projects ought to be undertaken to alleviate
the foreign-exchange situation, they cannot all be done at
once, because they temporarily increase the need for foreign exchange. The stock of efficient import-substitution
projects can be exploited only gradually, then, and some

kind of priority ranking among the alternatives must be made.[27]

In conclusion, once optimum expenditure policies are pursued, import substitution is in all probability the only way that import controls can be made effective and lead to any substantial curtailment of non-imput imports. But it is then necessary to ensure that only *efficient* import-substitution projects are undertaken and that they are made as efficient as possible. (Trade policy can be enlisted in a strategic manner to increase efficiency. See below, pp. 113-20.)

Measures to Increase Foreign-Exchange Earnings on Current Account

There are, in principle, two different ways that a developing country can increase its supply of foreign exchange on current account: (1) by shifting the domestic supply curves of exports, and (2) by shifting the foreign-demand curves for imports.

Shifting the Domestic Export Supply Curves

With given foreign-demand curves for imports, the obvious commercial-policy task on the export side is to manipulate the supply curves of exports so as to maximize foreign-exchange earnings.[28] There are two important considerations that must be observed in this context. They concern (1) the need for input imports to produce exports and (2) the elasticity of foreign demand for imports.

The requirement of input imports to produce exports means that there is an efficiency criterion of the same kind as the one relating to import substitution.[29] For a particular export project being evaluated, the criterion could be expressed in the following form:

$$M_e + tM_o < X.$$

If both sides are divided by X, the criterion would take the form:

$$r < 1.$$

If an investment for an export project has already been made, operations should be continued to the extent that the following, less strict criterion is fulfilled:

$$tM_O < X$$

or, if both sides are divided by X,

$$p < 1.$$

Since efficiency is likely to change through time, the appropriate time period on the basis of which the efficiency of an undertaking should be assessed, need not, any more than in the case of import substitution be its lifetime. Again, the most important consideration is the unavoidable initial inefficiency during the construction phase. Because of it, efficient export projects cannot be realized all at once, but must be ranked in order of priority. Indeed, there must be a coordination of import-substitution and export projects into one priority ranking.

The elasticity of the foreign demand for imports is important because developing countries export primary commodities to such a large extent. As soon as the foreign demand curve is not infinitely elastic, the foreign-exchange earnings of a particular export project must be corrected, not only for the foreign exchange used on input imports, but also for the foreign-exchange losses through lower prices on the existing export volume. In other words, the export value to be introduced into the efficiency criterion must express the marginal foreign-exchange revenue, this value being lower than the average foreign-exchange revenue, and, of course, the average revenue when demand is less than infinitely elastic.

The argument, as well as the equilibrium condition, may be expressed diagrammatically. In Figure 5, prices in terms of foreign currency are measured on the vertical axis, and the quantity supplied of a particular export product on the horizontal axis. A foreign-demand curve (Df) has been drawn. The first consideration relating to the input-import requirement for producing exports means that this demand curve must be corrected in such a way that a net foreign-exchange average revenue curve is obtained. For each sales volume, a point can be plotted at a certain distance below the demand curve, this distance representing unit outlays on input imports at the particular production volume. If all such points are connected, a locus is obtained. This locus (AR_f^n) is the relevant demand curve, i.e., the demand curve for the value added by domestic factors. As this particular locus has been drawn in the diagram, the unit outlays on input imports are assumed to be constant, irrespective of the production volume. The locus therefore runs below, and parallel to, the demand curve.

The efficiency condition first formulated requires that the AR_f^n curve run through the northeastern quadrant. However, and this is the second consideration, as soon as this curve is less than infinitely elastic, it is not enough that the export value exceeds the input-import requirement. This condition would be fulfilled up to a sales quantity of Oh. Instead, the optimum sales volume is where the elasticity of the net average revenue curve is unitary. Net foreign-exchange earnings will be maximized if the supply curve is manipulated so that it intersects the locus at this point. By drawing a marginal foreign-exchange revenue curve (MR_f^n), the optimum sales volume can be found at the particular point where this marginal curve intersects the horizontal axis. It should be observed that the appropriate commercial-policy measure to be applied may, in many cases, be an export restriction.

In Figure 5, the optimum sales volume is Oc. Total foreign-exchange receipts are cd times Oc, and net foreign-exchange receipts are cb times Oc. It should be noted that this diagram refers only to one particular export product. An aggregate foreign-demand curve cannot be used, because it would be an extreme coincidence

Figure 5

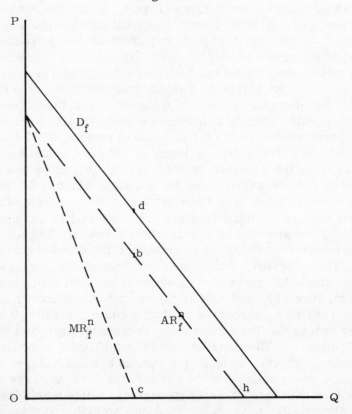

if one exchange rate, or rate of subsidy, or tax made all supply curves intersect all net demand curves at the special point of unitary elasticity. Thus, since the foreign-exchange supply curve of Figure 4 is an aggregate curve drawn on conventional assumptions, its zero elasticity point will most likely not express the maximum supply of foreign exchange that can be achieved if different com-mercial-policy measures are applied to the various export products. If, for instance, a system of multiple exchange rates is not introduced or is found impracticable, the calculations of net marginal foreign-exchange revenue must take into account the effects on the supply of foreign exchange of variations in the supply of all export products and not just of one export product at a time.

In order to contrast the commercial-policy theory being formulated with conventional theory, it should, at this stage, be pointed out that the optimum-tariff argument cannot be accepted. It has already been noted, when discussing import policies, that noninput imports are not restricted to improve the terms of trade and that input imports would not be restricted even if terms-of-trade gains could be achieved. It can now be added that exports should not be held back or stimulated to improve the (barter) terms of trade. Instead, they should be encouraged or discouraged in order to maximize what may be referred to as the "net income terms of trade." These terms of trade would measure the capacity to make input imports after having deducted those input imports which are required for export production. Any point where a trade indifference curve is tangent to the foreign-offer curve—i.e., the point at which the offer curve of the particular country imposing the optimum tariff should intersect the foreign-offer curve—is thus without relevance in the framework suggested here.

Shifting the Foreign-Demand Curves

No part of the commercial policy of developing countries can be pursued without considering the reaction of the advanced countries. If import-recomposition and export-promotion policies lead to retaliation in the advanced countries, the result may be a deterioration in the situation for the developing countries. But, apart from creating an understanding for their policies, developing countries face the more demanding task of persuading advanced countries to institute a nonreciprocal dismantling of their trade barriers on products of interest to developing countries. All in all, the developing countries must thus try to obtain a removal of foreign-trade barriers that is not only nonreciprocated but also combined with an acceptance of their unconventional commercial-policy measures.

There are many reasons for trade barriers used by advanced countries, most of them representing considerations of political expediency rather than economic rationality. But, the important fact here is that the advanced countries apply conventional trade theory in weighing their political and economic interests. Thus, an inappropriate theory of trade is used to determine commercial policies pursued vis-à-vis the developing countries. A reformulation of trade theory is for this reason of more than academic interest.

This situation, of conflicting theories of trade policy applied simultaneously in different groups of countries, can perhaps be illustrated in two payoff matrices. The first sets out the various alternatives as they emerge in the theory suggested here, and the second states the alternatives according to conventional theory.

Payoff Matrix 1 (Foreign-Exchange-Gap Theory)			Payoff Matrix 2 (Conventional Theory)	
Policy Combination	D_F	D_R	D_F	D_R
A_F	10, 10	10, 15	10, 10	8, 11
A_R	9, 5	9, 7-13	11, 8	9, 9

The letter A stands for advanced countries, and D for developing countries. The subscript F signifies free trade, and the subscript R implies some set of restrictions or subsidies, or both, which can be considered to be optimum according to the particular trade theory applied. (This optimum is judged according to a criterion of national, rather than world, welfare.) The first figure in each box refers to the payoff to advanced countries of a particular combination of policies; the second figure refers to the payoff to developing countries of the same combination of policies.

In Matrix 1, the $A_F D_R$ alternative represents an improvement for developing countries and no deterioration for advanced countries, compared with the double free-trade case. The developing countries gain, and gain substantially, from changing the composition of imports, and the advanced countries do not lose from this because the volume of total imports does not decrease. Contrary to what can be concluded on the basis of conventional theory, total payoff has thus increased. If, instead, advanced countries restrict their imports and developing countries pursue a free-trade policy, the latter will lose heavily, owing to reduced import opportunities in the wake of falling exports. The advanced countries may or may not gain, depending upon whether improved terms of trade more than offset a deterioration in allocation. It should be noted that the optimum tariff is more likely than not to be a zero tariff for the advanced countries and that any restrictions would thus lead to losses. This is so because the advanced countries would, at the same time, clamp on restrictions *among themselves*, assuming the restrictions to be applied on a most-favored-nation basis. As these tariffs will only lead to an inferior allocation, a net loss is very likely. In the matrix, a loss has been indicated. Total payoff is, in any case, reduced in comparison with the double free-trade case.

If both groups of countries apply restrictions, the payoff to advanced countries will not be affected in comparison with the case when they alone apply restrictions. This is so because the developing countries do not use their restrictions to reduce total imports, but to change the composition of imports.[30] As to the payoff to developing countries in this alternative, it may be *higher or lower* than in the double free-trade case. If the restrictions applied by the advanced countries are insignificant, it is likely that the recomposition of imports will bring gains outweighing the losses from the reduction in export proceeds. Thus, it is possible—and this is an interesting difference from conventional theory—that total payoff is higher when all countries apply restrictions than when all pursue free trade. However, even if this is the case, the payoff to the developing countries, as well as total payoff, must be smaller than in the $A_F D_R$ alternative.

The developing countries interpret the trade-policy situation in terms of this matrix, perhaps more through intuition than on the basis of an explicit theory. They feel they have a strong case in asking for the right to apply restrictions vis-à-vis advanced countries while, at the same time asking that the latter apply no restrictions against them. They recognize that the advanced countries *may*, but are not likely to, lose somewhat from the non-application of trade barriers. Under all circumstances, the gains for the developing countries would be much higher, leading to an increase in total gains. However, the advanced countries may impose trade barriers that they are prepared to abolish only through reciprocal concessions. Even in this case, the developing countries may find, if the obstacles applied by advanced countries are not too severe, that it is in their interest, not to negotiate, but to apply restrictions themselves in order to recompose their imports.

The advanced countries, on the other hand, interpret the policy situation in terms of Matrix 2, where there is no reason to put developing countries in any special category. Total payoff is maximized in the double free-trade alternative, while unilateral application of trade obstacles will, if constructed in an optimum form, benefit one party but reduce total payoff. Apart from various noneconomic reasons, the advanced countries may well prefer to continue to apply restrictions in order to offer an inducement to the developing countries to participate in a mutually beneficial reciprocal elimination of trade obstacles—at tariff conferences, for instance. True enough, they feel that the developing countries are likely to gain from improved terms of trade if the advanced countries abolish their trade obstacles unilaterally, but total payoff, they argue, would be even greater if there were reciprocity. And as commercial assistance to developing countries in the form of nonreciprocal concessions is but one part of a total assistance effort, it would be better to pursue policies that maximize total payoff, thereby forming a stronger basis for the over-all aid effort.

Of course, this presentation offers an extremely simplified picture of the considerations guiding policy-makers in the two groups of countries. For instance, if actual trade policies in developing countries are inefficient according to the criteria already formulated, or if expenditure policies are inappropriate, there may be a case for inducing them to make reciprocal concessions. But, the simplifications do bring out the conflict summed up in the two rival matrices. Of course, there may be a certain clash of interest between advanced and developing countries in the theory of trade policy underlying Matrix 1, too. However, an acceptance of this theory in the advanced countries—i.e., to the extent it can be proved to have analytical relevance—would change the present situation in many respects. Most important, it would become clear that a unilateral dismantling of trade barriers by the advanced countries is a less expensive form of aid to developing countries than other forms. The reverse conclusion emerges from conventional theory.

To the extent that theory has any influence on policy, it is to be expected that the trade policies of advanced countries show little evidence of an understanding of the trade requirements of developing countries. It may be of interest to assess the actual situation in this respect and to see what efforts have been made by the developing countries to influence the commercial policies of the advanced countries. In this context, it is convenient to distinguish between efforts and achievements within the *conventional* GATT machinery and those made through new approaches—inside and outside GATT.[31]

Some fifty (i.e., two-thirds) of all underdeveloped countries have joined GATT, either to make use of its conventional machinery, as constructed on the basis of the blueprints of neoclassical trade theory, or to obtain a forum for the advancement of ideas on new commercial-policy approaches. If we first examine how developing countries can benefit from the conventional GATT provisions, we note that GATT member countries assume certain obligations vis-à-vis one another. (1) No member may maintain any manmade trade barriers except tariffs and equilvalent charges. (2) Trade obstacles must be operated in a nondiscriminatory fashion. (3) Through reciprocal concessions, attempts should be made at tariff conferences to negotiate the removal or reduction of tariff obstacles. (4) To the extent tariff obstacles have been reduced or eliminated, they must not be reintroduced or increased during the period covered by the specific agreement. The developing countries can thus obtain what amounts to a series of commercial treaties with the advanced countries, under which their exports are not to be hampered be quantitative restrictions and tariff obstacles are negotiable.

This method of moving the foreign-demand curves out to the right has certain weaknesses, however. To begin with, a developing country assumes certain obligations with respect to its own commercial policy, which may make it more difficult to free foreign exchange for input imports and to promote exports. In practice, however, the obligations have not at all proved extensive. A major reason for this is that contrary to the teachings of theory, the advanced countries themselves, have, for internal political reasons, wanted to be able to maintain temporary restrictions in case of balance-of-payments troubles, and the underdeveloped countries have been able to make extensive use of the provision for balance-of-payments restrictions to handle their own problems.[32] But the reason why it has been easy to escape the obligations has also weakened the advantages as the advanced countries have, in various ways, not lived up to their obligations. For instance, they have not eliminated all their quantitative restrictions even in cases where these could not be defended on balance-of-payments grounds.[33]

A third disadvantage is that the developing countries have not been able to make much use of the provisions for tariff negotiations. There have been five tariff conferences.[34] At these conferences, underdeveloped countries have concluded 215 tariff agreements with advanced countries and 31 agreements among themselves, a total of 246. This is a very small number compared to the number of agreements that could have been concluded and to the number of agreements concluded by advanced countries. Furthermore, in spite of there being more and more underdeveloped member countries in GATT, the number of agreements concluded has sharply declined, particularly agreements among underdeveloped countries. At the two most recent conferences, a total of 39 agreements were made by underdeveloped countries, all of which with advanced countries.[35] And the scope of the agreements concluded by underdeveloped countries seems comparatively limited.[36]

Some of the reasons why developing countries have not participated more actively in the tariff conferences are as follows:

1. The basis for the tariff negotiations is the rule of reciprocity. To negotiate away foreign tariff obstacles, a developing country would have to assume certain obligations in its own tariff policy.

2. Quite a few of the trade obstacles, although in principle negotiable, have proved non-negotiable. This has been the case with various fiscal charges, for instance.

3. The negotiation rules have stipulated that, for a country to be able to initiate talks on a concession for a particular product, it must be a "principal supplier" or have a "substantial interest" in the export trade of that product. As developing countries are not usually in that position, except with respect to various raw materials (for which there are few tariff obstacles), they have often been unable to negotiate.

4. The negotiation machinery has been too complicated for developing countries wishing to use their administrative manpower for other purposes. The conferences are time-consuming and expensive as well. Since a considerable part of the expenses had been in foreign exchange, this aspect of the conferences is probably particularly unattractive.

It is not surprising, then, that the developing countries have not made greater use of the negotiation provisions of GATT. The advantages they have derived from these negotiations stem from the indirect benefits accruing from concessions negotiated between advanced countries and extended to all member countries, thanks to the most-favored-nation clause.

In sum, neither the theory nor the workings of the *original* GATT machinery has proved to be a sufficiently suitable or powerful means of increasing demand for the exports of developing countries. Anything else would, indeed, be surprising, since the original GATT doctrine was based on a concept of commercial policy emanating from a trade theory that has been found inapplicable to developing countries.

However, new approaches to the export problems of developing countries have been tried. Until the U.N. Conference on Trade and Development (UNCTAD) of 1964, these efforts were concentrated in GATT, most of this work being done by the so-called Committee III, set up in 1958 under a Program for Expansion of International Trade. The main activities of Committee III have been: requesting developing countries to list products they are interested in exporting; surveying all trade obstacles that hamper exports of these products; urging the speedy removal of such trade obstacles in developed countries; and reviewing the progress made in the elimination of such trade obstacles.

To render the efforts more effective, an Action Program was adopted in the spring of 1963, containing the following seven points. (These still give an adequate picture of what the underdeveloped countries are trying to achieve at the negotiation table.)

1. The maintenance of a "standstill" on new tariff and nontariff barriers.

2. The elimination of quantitative restrictions by the end of 1965.

3. The introduction of duty-free entry of tropical products by the end of 1963.

4. The elimination of tariffs on primary products.

5. The elimination, or at least reduction, of tariffs on exports of semiprocessed and processed products over a three-year period.

6. The progressive reduction of internal fiscal charges and revenue duties.

7. Annual reporting on the implementation of the Action Program.

Through the addition, in 1965, of a new chapter to GATT, embodying these demands of the underdeveloped countries, the advanced countries have shown that they have found it at least politically expedient to accept the underdeveloped countries' assessment of the role of trade. However, even if they have duly cooperated in GATT in formulating such policy goals, they have not participated with the sense of urgency that one would expect would come from a real reinterpretation of the role of trade for developing countries. On the whole, they have limited their actions to a passive acceptance of whatever commercial-policy measures the developing countries have chosen to take. They have also offered to conduct the Kennedy Round —if it is conducted at all—without any demands for reciprocity from the developing countries. This is perhaps not much of a concession; if the developing countries choose not to participate in the Round, the very construction of GATT on the principle of nondiscrimination would mean that the tariff cuts would have to be extended to them anyhow. There has not been, it must be concluded, a sufficient change of mood reflecting awareness of the different role trade is being given in the developing countries; substantial trade obstacles remain, even if some progress in the lowering of trade barriers for goods of interest to developing countries can, no doubt, be noted.[37]

Dissatisfaction among the developing countries over the achievements of GATT, and increasing awareness of the importance of trade in the development efforts, led to the convocation of UNCTAD. It is, as yet, too early to judge the achievements of this conference. However, even if its concrete results have, so far, been no more than the creation of a piece of new machinery, and even if it is *a new mentality and not new machinery* that is needed, the conference itself and future ones may contribute to a wider understanding of the trade problems of developing countries, eventually leading to greater progress there or within GATT.

Measures to Bridge a Foreign-Exchange Gap Through Capital-Account Transactions

> *"If in the past the Indian budgets were a gamble in the rains, today Indian plans are a gamble in international charity."*
> *—P.K. Bardhan* [38]

More foreign exchange for input imports can be mobilized in ways affecting the capital account.

1. *Prevention of an accumulation of capital assets abroad.* A capital outflow for business purposes from the developing country may or may not be deemed advantageous. But there may also be an unequivocally disadvantageous capital flight due to political insecurity or economic difficulties. There are two kinds of the latter arising from the foreign-exchange problem itself. First, the efforts to reserve foreign exchange for input imports, and the controls on non-input imports that are required for this purpose, will make it attractive to accumulate foreign assets for consumption abroad. This kind of evasion must be taken into account when assessing the efficiency of import controls. Second, it is possible that a looming frustration of savings, caused by a deficiency of foreign exchange for input imports, could lead to a capital flight. A prospective investor, not expecting to be able to procure the input imports he needed, might, evading the controls, divert foreign exchange for investment abroad. Thus, it is conceivable that there is a vicious circle, where lack of foreign exchange leads to a capital outflow, which results in an even greater deficiency of

foreign exchange, and so on, making the final frustration of savings greater than need be.

2. *Running down capital assets abroad.* One interesting category of such assets is foreign-exchange reserves. In spite of a foreign-exchange gap, reserves accumulated during preceding periods may be available for use. The country may have not faced a foreign-exchange gap earlier, or it may have substituted internal for external equilibrium. Another situation in which developing countries may run down reserves is when there have been institutional changes reducing the *need* for reserves—for instance, if some operative scheme for commodity price stabilization had been adopted, or if an international body had instituted a system of "compensatory finance," i.e., *ex-post* in-payments and out-payments that even out the effects on foreign-exchange receipts of fluctuations in commodity prices.[39]

3. *Acceptance of, and pressure for, aid.*[40]   It is convenient to distinguish between outright aid in the form of money or in kind, and the transfer of funds through the adoption of certain quasi-commercial policies in the advanced countries. Aid would include not only the obvious forms of aid but also, for instance, the amount of subsidization inherent in so-called soft loans. It would also include the net aid effect of export and foreign-investment insurance schemes operated by advanced countries to support their exporters and investors on such terms that the arrangements are to be regarded not as insurance schemes proper but as a kind of subsidization. This aid differs from the ordinary type in that only in retrospect can one see which transactions in fact were aid and which were regular business. Some forms of aid would be included only to the extent they relieve balance-of-payments pressures. For instance, military aid may or may not save foreign exchange. The same is true of the disposal of agricultural surpluses, because the agricultural products might be producible at home and the disposal of them may depress the prices of certain export products.[41] Another kind of surplus disposal—of economically

depreciated capital equipment—is interesting primarily because offers of such disposal have evidently been regularly turned down by developing countries. This suggests that the psychological explanation of the input-import factor-proportions problem is very important: nothing but equipment embodying the most advanced technology is attractive, and it must be imported and paid for.

As to aid in the form of quasi-commercial policies adopted by the advanced countries, there are two variants: commodity agreements that lift the general price level, rather than stabilize prices around the free-market trend; and compensatory financing, beyond a mere insurance against price fluctuations. These measures must be considered as aid, in spite of the fact that many regard the fall that has been supposed to have taken place in commodity prices as "unfair" or even "immoral." The heated debate on the question whether or not the terms of trade have deteriorated for underdeveloped countries seems irrelevant. The important fact is simply that the terms of trade are not *good enough* to prevent the underdeveloped countries from having to face difficult trade problems.

4. *Creation of conditions favorable to borrowing.* Borrowing would include both foreign direct investment and portfolio investment.

When studied within the analytical framework applied here, these capital-account transactions give rise to a number of important problems. In the following discussion, they will be grouped under two headings: problems referring to the "optimum time path" of spending foreign-exchange funds, including the problem of foreign-exchange reserve adequacy; and problems referring to the efficiency of the measures in question, one aspect of which is the well-known servicing problem.

The Optimum Time Path of Spending Foreign Exchange

A question that requires careful consideration is how available funds of accommodating finance should be used over time. Assume, for instance, that a country has some

excess foreign-exchange reserves that can be used to fill
an exchange gap. The problem is whether these funds
should be used right away, during the first period, or
whether their use should be spaced out over a number of
periods. The answer is that, under certain circumstances,
it is wasteful to use all the funds during the original
period—when expansion imports are financed to such an
extent that sufficient maintenance imports—needed to prevent the new capacity from standing idle—cannot be secured during subsequent periods.

If certain assumptions are made, it is possible to iso-
late a situation for which the optimum spending path of
certain funds of foreign exchange can be discussed more
precisely. Assume: (1) that a developing country has a
certain amount of excess foreign-exchange reserves;
(2) that there are stationary and stable foreign-exchange
earnings on current account and that capital-account
transactions result in a constant net balance; (3) that there
are some projects to be financed that do not lead to any
new exports or to any import substitution; and (4) that
the country is indifferent to the time distribution of additional income. It is then possible to formulate a spending
criterion, stating that the volume of expansion imports in
the first period should be exactly so large that the remaining foreign-exchange reserves suffice to procure all
operation imports necessary to keep the investments
made by the expansion imports fully employed during
their whole life. The optimum condition could then be
written:

$$M_e + t a M_e = K,$$

or:

$$M_e (1 + t a) = K,$$

where M_e is the expansion imports, t is the lifetime of
the investment in periods, a is the fraction of operation
imports required in one period divided by expansion imports (M_o/M_e), and K is the excess reserves (including
any interest accruing if those reserves that have not yet
been spent are invested on the international money mar-

kets). If this criterion is fulfilled, no capacity will be left idle during its life. If the criterion is not fulfilled and there are excessive expansion imports during the first period, there will be subsequent unemployment of capacity. It is interesting, in this context, to note the present Indian overcapacity after a period of running down excess reserves.

If the assumptions are modified, the criterion will have to be modified accordingly. If the fourth assumption is changed so that there is assumed to be a preference for earlier income rather than later, the expansion imports would have to be larger. This would lead to higher income during the first periods, but to lower total income because of wasted capacity in later periods. If the project in question leads to some exports or import substitution, the initial expansion imports will also be higher. This case, a modification of the third assumption, could be analytically handled by redefining K to include the foreign exchange earned through the exports or the import substitution. It should be noted that, if the project to be financed qualifies as efficient, the problem of the optimum spending path disappears. This is because the realization of the project itself will create scope for the maintenance imports it requires. Let us also consider a modification of the second assumption, i.e., a case in which the amount of accommodating finance available is not an *ad hoc* phenomenon. Any such subsequent amounts would also have to be treated as additions to K and would call for higher expansion imports during the first period.

At this stage, the problem of an optimum spending path may be broadened by assuming irregular earnings of foreign exchange, either on current or capital account, instead of a given fund to be spent. The problem at hand now becomes identical to that of holding an *optimum amount of foreign-exchange reserves*.

During an upturn in earnings, capacity may be added that cannot be supplied with operation imports during a downturn in earnings. To avoid this danger, it is necessary for the country to hold foreign-exchange reserves.

The motive for foreign-exchange reserves in conventional theory is that they act as a buffer, obviating the necessity of making adjustments in expenditure policies when there are short-term variations in exports and imports, and enabling the country to make gradual adjustments to long-term changes. In the theory suggested here, the reason for holding foreign-exchange reserves is, for a developing country, very different. It is to avoid waste of capacity due to changes in foreign-exchange earnings—a waste that *cannot be avoided,* even if the country tried to adjust its expenditure policies to the changes in foreign-exchange earnings. Whereas in conventional theory the motive for holding reserves is not so strong that it has not been possible to question it, it is extremely strong in the alternative theory, owing to the leverage effect on capacity use that would follow from shifts in foreign-exchange earnings.[42] Furthermore, whereas the case against holding *excess* reserves is not particularly strong in conventional theory, it is very strong in our theory, because the excess reserves, if used, would have a leverage effect on capacity use and growth.

Thus, the adoption of a sound criterion for reserve adequacy and adherence to this criterion are extremely important for developing countries. In practice, it is likely that reserves become too small. This occurs because it is easy to spend existing reserves, but not to create them when they are needed. Underdeveloped countries complain about instability in export earnings, in spite of the fact that industrialization seems to be no cure for export instability.[43] Their complaints are easy to understand, however, against the background of the negative leverage effects of the recurrent deficiency of foreign exchange in combination with inadequate reserves. For this reason, it would be advantageous if the reserve-holding function could be institutionalized through a system of compensatory finance or made largely unnecessary through commodity price stabilization. Both these kinds of measures are referred to here not in their capacity as quasi-commercial policies for aid transfers but as measures for evening out *shifts* in foreign-exchange earnings.

The Problem of Servicing

Prevention of capital outflow and stimulation of capital inflow in the form of borrowing have to be efficient in the same sense as measures to control imports and to promote exports must be. The measures in question must result in a real improvement in the foreign-exchange-gap situation.[44]

Measures to prevent capital outflow could become inefficient either because they create domestic conditions providing an additional reason for trying to build up foreign assets (and, as such controls are difficult to administer, they might actually increase the capital flight) or because they make it more difficult to stimulate a capital *inflow* from other sources.

With respect to measures to stimulate borrowing, the efficiency problem arises out of the necessity to service certain types of capital imports. The service charges are a form of input-import requirement for operation purposes. To the extent that capital imports require servicing, they thus increase the import minimum—in case of interest payments on top of amortization, by an amount exceeding the capital inflow. The efficiency problem at hand is thus identical to the servicing problem that has received so much attention during recent years.

In a study of the servicing problem, the starting point must be the observation already made in the chapter on theory that, for the same reasons that the role of *trade* is different from what it is in conventional theory, the role of *capital imports* differs from the role assigned them in conventional theory. In conventional theory, capital imports serve the sole function of supplementing domestic savings in order to make possible a higher rate of investment than could be realized without reducing domestic consumption. In the framework presented in this

study, capital imports that help to bridge a foreign-exchange gap supplement not insufficient domestic savings,
but insufficient foreign-exchange resources, which must
be augmented in order to avoid making the domestic
savings superfluous. Beyond the closing of a foreign-exchange gap, capital imports serve the conventional function.

The reason for the difference between ordinary capital
imports and capital imports that bridge a foreign-exchange gap is acutely relevant to the servicing problem.
In conventional theory, capital imports take place to avoid
a contraction of domestic expenditure required *now* so as
to cut back expenditure at a *later stage*, when, at a higher
income level, it can be done more conveniently. Technically, it is a matter of operating the "transfer mechanism." Servicing difficulties must be due to a lack of
willingness, and not of capacity, to service. However,
within the analytical framework used here, the matter is
not so simple. It is conceivable that, for the very same
reasons that capital imports are necessary to avoid the
negative effects of an unclosed foreign-exchange gap,
capital imports made now might be impossible to service
later *without cutting back input imports and widening a
still prevailing foreign-exchange gap*. In the case of developing countries, capital imports must be made because
a contraction in domestic expenditure would be of no
avail in securing the required foreign-exchange resources. For the same reason, obtaining the foreign exchange necessary to service the loans need not be a simple
matter of appropriate expenditure policies in the future.
As service charges are a kind of operation imports, and
must be included when calculating the future need for input
imports, capital imports might thus be a way of avoiding
a foreign-exchange gap now only to face an aggravated
gap at a later stage.

The implications of this are as follows. From a welfare point of view, there might appear to be a stronger
case for capital imports in the trade theory suggested
here. But the situation is, rather, that the case for *cer-*

tain forms of capital imports is strengthened, while the case for other forms is not necessarily stronger and may even be weaker. The types of capital imports that are unequivocally beneficial and that can turn trade into an actual superengine of growth, and not only a frustrating potential superengine, are those which do not give rise to any service charges. To this category belong aid and utilization of excess reserves.

Borrowing, however, might not help the country any more than as a temporary relief with negative future consequences. There is a condition that is both necessary and sufficient to guarantee that the future situation will not deteriorate through the borrowing: that, after regular earnings have been used in the most appropriate way, the loans will be used to finance projects that earn foreign exchange through increased exports or import substitution in an *efficient* way. It will be remembered from the discussion of import substitution and export promotion that there may be efficient projects that cannot be realized, owing to the foreign-exchange cost of the initial investments. If such projects still qualify as efficient *even when charged with the service costs, which have to be included in the operation imports*, the initial foreign-exchange costs for expansion imports can be financed by borrowing, without future servicing problems and cutbacks in input imports. This is obviously a sufficient condition for borrowing to be beneficial. It is also necessary, however. As long as regular foreign-exchange earnings are used in the most appropriate way and the country still suffers from a foreign-exchange gap, financing inefficient projects will lead to a future deterioration in the situation through future service charges. The approach to the merits of capital imports must be on a *project basis*, as long as the over-all effects of investments do not remove the foreign-exchange gap altogether.

The fact that the projects must be efficient even when service costs are added to the operation imports means that the terms of the loans are of great importance. The lower the interest rate, the lower the addition to operation imports which the project must bear; and the longer the repayment period, the later the project needs to earn foreign exchange to repay principal. The concept "soft loans" can be defined more closely, and the need for such loans identified more precisely, in terms of the trade theory outlined here than in terms of conventional theory. The only sign of recognition given this problem by conventional theory is a loose reference to the difficulty of servicing loans on commercial terms at a low income level.

A country borrowing to finance an efficient project faces the interesting problem of *how much* should be borrowed. The International Bank for Reconstruction and Development (IBRD) has based its activities on the doctrine of lending the "foreign-exchange content" of the project, leaving it to the borrowing country to finance the rest of the cost domestically. This policy has been much criticized.[45] It has been argued on conventional grounds that there is no reason, or that it is at least arbitrary, to make a distinction between the foreign-exchange component and the non-foreign-exchange component of a project. If a country could not adjust its expenditure policies accordingly, it would need to borrow the full amount. On the other hand, if it could pursue stricter expenditure policies, it could create scope for the imports needed to realize the project. There would thus be no need to borrow at all. Under the pressure of this kind of criticism of its policy, it appears that the IBRD has been changing over to the attitude that it may lend a much higher percentage than the foreign-exchange content of a project.[46]

The theory discussed here suggests, however, that it would be sufficient to lend only the foreign-exchange content. Once a country has this foreign exchange, it can use available domestic resources to realize the project without any extra difficulties in curtailing expenditure. This does not, of course, mean that the IBRD cannot serve the developing countries well by lending more than is needed for a particular project. The additional amounts could be used to procure operation imports during the first period of the project, when, in spite of its eventual foreign-exchange saving effects, scope for these operation imports might not yet have been created.

One implication of the argument concerning the repayment difficulties is that, for it to be possible to service a loan, it is not enough for a country that the projects financed by the loan yield profits or add to GNP. In conventional theory, this is enough, in the sense that it ensures that it will, in fact, be more convenient at a later stage to cut back expenditures because incomes have risen. This is the reason for the conventional insistence that the investments financed by borrowings must be "productive," a condition that is strengthened here by the requirement that the project must be an efficient saver of foreign exchange.

The proposition that income increases do not suffice to ensure repayment capacity bears on the role of direct investment from abroad. On the basis of conventional theory, it can be maintained that repayment is even more easily handled in the case of direct investments than in the case of portfolio investments: either the investment is profitable, and then there is scope for the servicing; or the investment is not profitable, and then there is no need for servicing. The latter part of this observation remains true within the alternative trade theory, but the former part is not necessarily correct. The direct investment may well be profitable without earning or saving foreign exchange, and direct investment can thus lead to servicing problems. This does not mean that direct investment is to be discouraged, but, that in order to avoid future conflicts with foreign investors, there must be guarantees that the direct investments lead either to efficient import substitution or to exports.

It might thus be best to discontinue the present emphasis on domestic growth as a sufficient condition for the equilibrating forces to operate and create scope for service payments. It should, instead, be argued that capital imports that are not requited, and thus give rise to *no* service charges, function to bridge a foreign-exchange gap and have strong beneficial effects. On the other hand, capital imports that have to be serviced must have a positive effect on the foreign-exchange position, either through efficient import substitution or through a direct increase in exports, in order to be useful. Otherwise, capital imports represent a mere postponement, and a disadvantageous one, of the gap problem. A gap is closed today only to open up all the more tomorrow. Such capital imports will lead to an initial growth in domestic income, owing to the increase in input imports financed by the loans. If there have been no direct positive effects on the foreign-exchange situation, this growth, instead of being a sufficient condition for successful servicing, will disappear when service charges reduce the scope for input imports. The present rapid rise in "debt-service ratios" (the ratio between debt-service charges and current-account earnings) is alarming, in that it might indicate that developing countries have overestimated their repayment capacity and are presently borrowing to pay service costs.[47] This is a process that will have one of the following results: First, it may lead to default, i.e., a cutback of a particular kind of input imports; this will, however, make it hard to borrow in the future, even for efficient projects. Second, it may result in a curtailment of other forms of input imports in order to pay service charges.

We thus have two conflicting interpretations of repayment capacity, the one following from the role assigned capital imports in conventional theory, and the other a consequence of the role given these imports in our alternative theory. Against this background, it is interesting to look at the literature on the repayment problem of developing countries, the "pathology of international capital flows,"[48] as it has been aptly called. This literature is chiefly inspired by IBRD and consists of a number of works that are analytical without necessarily being short-hand applications of conventional theory.[49] In fact, the approach to the repayment problem shows an interesting change through time.

The first of these contributions is essentially based

on conventional theory. According to Alter, "It is clear that there is nothing in the economic mechanism as such which makes it impossible to adjust the claims on total resources, on saving, and on foreign exchange, so that debt service payments can be met. This is true either under the assumption of the gold standard and the classical adjustment mechanism or under the modern panoply of fiscal and monetary policy with or without direct controls."[50] He then observes that in reality there are, however, a variety of rival claims on the resources. Under strain, a developing country might, for political reasons, be unable to pursue policies that leave sufficient room for debt servicing. The strains can be either short-term, such as fluctuations in export earnings, or long-term, such as a slower rate of growth than expected. Alter stresses, in particular, the importance of a high rate of per-capita income growth as a condition for economic policies that ensure sufficient scope for debt servicing.

He thus argues that, in practice, there might be servicing difficulties due to balance-of-payments strains of the same kind that advanced countries experience under present conditions. In other words, the developing countries are said to face those adjustment problems that have led economists like Mundell to characterize the present balance-of-payments system in general as a "disequilibrium system," in contrast to the classical automatic adjustment. However, these adjustment problems arise because, the forces of adjustment are, for political reasons, not allowed to become active. According to Alter, adjustment is possible, if only it were possible to pursue optimal expenditure policies.

From this position, the approach within the IBRD seems to have changed considerably—and in a direction that lends support to the implications for the repayment problem of the trade analysis undertaken here. This is true, even if the most recent of the papers takes the same basic position as Alter.[51]

If the rate of increase in real income and savings, remaining available after the claims of foreign capital have been met, is reasonably high, if growth occurs in a continuous fashion, and if its benefits are widespread, it can plausibly be argued that debt service payments will also be made smoothly. In this case, the opportunity cost of fulfilling external obligations is less obvious and presumably less burdensome, than in a situation in which service payments impinge on existing living standards and employment levels. Therefore, it can be argued—and this is the fundamental judgment on which this study rests—that continuing growth in per-capita production and the underlying process of rapid accumulation of productive capital is the basic long-run condition of debt servicing capacity.[52]

From this statement, it might appear that the prime concern is still to formulate conditions under which the policy situation is such that the equilibrating forces can be given free rein. However, the IBRD paper goes on to introduce a number of elements that are more easily fitted into our approach than into the conventional one:

1. The two concepts "compressible imports" and "minimum tolerable level of imports" are used to assess how much imports can be cut back in a balance-of-payments crisis to resolve the conflict between the rival use of resources in favor of debt servicing.[53] This distinction implies a factor-proportions problem.

2. The implications of direct foreign investment for debt-servicing capacity are also discussed. A distinction is made here between the investments typical of the past, which increased export capacity, and present-day investments, which are increasingly aimed at the markets of the developing country itself.[54] This distinction is meaningless within the conventional theory, but fits well into our framework.

3. In a digression on what is called the "adjustment problem," i.e., the problem of structural adjustment in the economy to transfer savings abroad, it is noted that considerable problems might be created by a deterioration in primary-commodity prices. In this situation, "various avenues of compensation are possible," such as productivity increases in primary production and a shift

of resources to new primary exports. Having outlined
these alternatives, the report continues:

> However, it is highly unlikely that the developing countries
> as a group can solve their long-run transfer problem only
> by cost reduction of existing primary exports or by develop-
> ing new ones. International demand for many primary
> products increases at a slower rate than imports of ma-
> terials and equipment required to sustain a satisfactory
> growth in income. Consequently, import substitution, chiefly
> in the industrial field, is the typical pattern of adjustment.[55]

This emphasis on import substitution and disregard of
the alternative adjustment through the exportation of
manufactures cannot be derived from conventional theory
and suggests an implicit reference to an export maximum.

4. In a discussion of the debt-servicing ratio, it is
pointed out that "foreign exchange is one of the scarcest,
if not the most scarce, inputs for the developing debtor
countries both over the short-run and over a longer period. The debt service is a continuing charge against this
scarce resource. It is an indicator, if again an incomplete
one, of the strength of the temptation to default."[56] This
quotation must be taken to mean that, according to IBRD,
developing countries face foreign-exchange gaps as defined here.

In view of these various elements that are creeping
into the IBRD analysis of the repayment problem, it is
tempting to conclude that support can be found for the
conclusions regarding the role of capital imports and
the repayment problem derived from the analytical framework used here.

TRADE POLICY AMONG DEVELOPING COUNTRIES AND
VIS-À-VIS BACKWARD COUNTRIES

In the final section of chapter 2, the conclusion was
drawn that a trade theory in terms of factor-proportions

problems, input imports, and foreign-exchange gaps was inapplicable to trade among developing countries. Instead, it was suggested that the conventional allocation theory of trade might offer a reasonably good approximation of the effects of the intratrade among developing countries. Thus, the commercial-policy principle to be pursued among developing countries would be free trade with conventional modifications. This policy could also be applied vis-à-vis backward countries. Under free trade, conditions for an optimum allocation of resources would be created, maximum benefits of large-scale production would be reaped, and the stimulus of competition would be insured. The static efficiency thus achieved would also promote dynamic efficiency, i.e., growth.

A Theory of Economic Integration

The suggestion that free trade might be the best principle to apply to trade relationships among developing countries and with backward countries means that for the developing countries two different commercial-policy *desiderata* must be met simultaneously. One refers to policies vis-à-vis the advanced countries, the other to policies vis-à-vis other developing countries and backward countries. To make this possible, the developing countries should have recourse to *economic integration*. After all, the formation of a customs union or a free-trade area means exactly this—a possibility to pursue free trade within one group of countries and, at the same time, retain whatever trade obstacles are deemed essential against another group of countries.[57]

If the extensive trade barriers that developing countries need in trade with advanced countries were extended on a most-favored-nation basis, the scope for trade with underdeveloped countries would be extremely limited. Since the domestic markets of most developing countries are small, the gains to be derived from the economic integration of such countries are thus considerable: the scope for improved allocation of existing resources, particularly of future additions to resources, would be great; economies of scale and advantages in the form of intensified competition would, in all likelihood, also be substantial; furthermore, it could offer the escape from the requirement of balanced growth—whether continuous balance, à la Nurkse, or "jigsaw balance," à la Hirschman. In fact, it might well be argued that it is absolutely necessary for a developing country to be able to derive, within a framework of economic integration, the allocation benefits from trade with other underdeveloped countries. To all these gains in the form of optimum allocation of present and future resources, large-scale production, and competition can be added a final, and most important, category of benefits. This is the possibility of achieving through integration greater efficiency in import substitution, and, in consequence, greater efficiency in export production.

As was pointed out in the discussion of import substitution, measures to substitute imports must be efficient—i.e., foreign-exchange-saving,—to have the desired effects. But conditions for efficiency may be hard to meet. It is most likely that the difficulties can be overcome more easily if each developing country does not try in isolation to substitute all non-input imports. It should be noted that, in a sense, the term "import substitution" may be misleading, giving the impression that a developing country, trying to reserve more foreign exchange for input imports through import restrictions, has to produce the efficient import substitutes *all by itself*, whereas what is needed is for the developing countries *as a group* to produce, and exchange among themselves, the non-input products that they formerly imported from developed countries.

It will be easier to achieve input substitution as a group because chances are greater that at least one of the countries has the capacity to produce attractive substitutes. This increased probability follows from the allocation approach itself, and on the contention that different countries have different qualifications for producing the various products, as well as from the advantages of economies of scale and competition. Through the advantages of improved allocation, efficient import substitution can take place in products already produced in at least one country; but economies of scale and intensified competition can lead to efficient import substitution in goods that no developing country could manage to produce in isolation.

Thus, all the general arguments in favor of free trade among developing countries also increase the prospects for the efficient substitution of imports from the advanced countries through economic integration. This also means that a better foundation is created for efficiency in export production. To the extent that trade between developing countries has these effects, the conventional forces behind the gains from trade will, in addition, exert a leverage effect on capacity use and growth in the developing countries through the greater availability of foreign exchange for input imports from advanced countries.

A New Customs-Union Theory Contrasted with the Neoclassical Customs-Union Theory

Paradoxically enough, the customs-union theory developed here, although derived from neoclassical trade theory, is very different from it. According to conventional theory, customs unions are beneficial to the extent that they lead to trade creation rather than trade diversion.[58] Trade creation arises when the elimination of the tariff walls between members in the union leads to the extinction of inefficient producers; owing to the destruction of a former element of discrimination between domestic and foreign sources of supply, new trade flows are created between the member countries. Trade diversion, on the other hand, occurs when goods that used to be imported from countries outside the union are now, owing to the new element of discrimination between union and nonunion sources of supply, imported from a member country. According to conventional customs-union theory, trade creation leads to an improved allocation of resources, whereas trade diversion leads to inferior allocation. The welfare effects of a particular customs union cannot be determined a priori.

This basic analysis, provided by Viner, has been extended in various ways. For instance, there might be some benefits from trade expansion due to the response to the lower prices that follow tariff elimination. But, there is no need to go into these refinements, since the theory suggested in this study differs basically from the conventional theory. As in conventional theory, trade creation in our theory is beneficial, leading to a superior allocation of resources. Trade diversion, however, is nothing but the manifestation of the success of additional efficient import substitution and is *not* detrimental. Indeed, to the extent that it consists of diverting imports of non-inputs away from advanced countries, it is a major objective of the customs union between the developing countries. It enables the concentration of scarce foreign exchange on input imports, thereby exerting a leverage on capacity use and growth. The question is not whether the new producer (in a member country) is less productive than the former one (in a nonmember country). Within the theoretical framework developed in this study, this question can be shown to amount to partial analysis. The question is, instead, whether it is not more advantageous to buy goods from the new producer than to use up foreign exchange by importing them from an advanced country. When making comparisons, one must broaden the analysis to take into account the effects on capacity use and growth of using the one or the other. The producer who, in a partial analysis, can be shown to be the relatively less productive can be proved to be the most economical when making a more general analysis. The gains from trade diversion could, in a sense, thus be said to *exceed* those of trade creation. From trade creation, the country derives the benefits of improved allocation, whereas trade diversion enables the country to free more foreign exchange for input imports, with a stimulating effect on capacity use and growth.[59]

It may be easier to see why trade diversion is beneficial if it is pointed out that the alternative to importing from a member country is not to import from the relatively more efficient producer in an advanced country, but to produce the good domestically. In all cases where it has proved possible to produce efficient import substitutes before the formation of the customs union, there will be scope for trade creation, in that the industry in question might prove competitive when the internal tariff barriers are abolished. It is in cases where the attempts at import substitution have proved futile that there will be scope for trade diversion. We can look at trade diversion as something that takes place when there is no scope for trade creation because the country has, in fact, not been able, on its own, to substitute imports from developed countries. The difference between "trade creation" and "trade diversion" is now almost nonexistent.

Thus, a customs union embracing the developing countries is an unmixed blessing, whereas a customs union of advanced countries has negative, as well as positive, effects, the balance of which is difficult to determine a priori.

Elaboration of the New Theory of Integration and Some Institutional Suggestions

So far, it has been assumed that economic integration takes the form of a customs union among all developing countries. Against the background of the theory developed on this assumption, it is interesting to discuss the effects of alternative forms of integration. The first question mark concerns *geographical scope*. It is important to note that a customs union can be regarded as an unmixed blessing for developing countries only if it comprises *all* developing countries. Otherwise, trade could be diverted from one country outside the union to another country inside the union—a form of diversion that would be of the conventional and harmful type. This kind of trade diversion would be harmful, as it means that conventional theory is being applied to the intratrade relationships of developing countries. In order to analyze the welfare effects of customs unions comprising fewer than all developing countries, we would have to use both the conventional customs-union theory and the new theory suggested here. All trade creation would be regarded as beneficial; trade diversion away from advanced countries would be beneficial; and trade diversion away from other developing countries would be detrimental. In order to estimate, a priori, the risks of trade diversion of the latter type, use would have to be made of the same sort of criteria as those employed to estimate the risks of trade diversion in conventional theory.

The standard criteria, or at least the most obvious ones, could be summarized as follows: the risks of trade diversion are smaller (1) the more competitive, rather than complementary, the economies of the integration partners; (2) the larger the union; (3) the more prohibitive the transport costs between member and nonmember countries; (4) the higher the original tariff walls; and (5) the lower the common external tariff.[60] The first four criteria could be adopted directly when estimating the risks of detrimental trade diversion in a union not embracing all developing countries. The fifth criterion is formally applicable; however, it must be borne in mind that low external trade obstacles, although reducing the risk of detrimental trade diversion, might prejudice the chances for beneficial trade diversion.

The next problem concerns the question of complete versus partial removal of trade obstacles among the developing countries, i.e., whether a preference arrangement among developing countries, rather than a customs union, could or could not be advantageous. In conventional commercial-policy theory, perferences are usually not looked upon as a recommendable system, the reason being a suspicion that preferences would, in practice, be awarded on products the increased importation of which would not threaten existing domestic production in one of the group. In other words, preferences would be given so that they would lead to no trade creation, but to much trade diversion. Although such preference systems would not be in the long-run economic interest of the participating countries, it is feared that they can be brought about by motives of short-run political expediency. That customs unions are accepted under the rules of GATT, whereas preferences are not permitted (except those preferences that already existed at the inception of GATT) is a reflection of this fear.

On the other hand, it has been argued by Meade that, to the extent they are given on all goods, preferences, as compared to the complete removal of trade obstacles, would reduce the risks of trade diversion more than the chances for trade creation. The reason for this is that a partial reduction of tariffs is likely to exhaust more than proportionally the full scope for trade creation, but only proportionally the full scope for trade diversion. [61]

Because of the different treatment in our new theory of the welfare effects of trade diversion in integration schemes embracing the developing countries, our conclusions on the effects of preferences differ from the conventional ones. A preference system involving no trade creation, but only trade diversion—not acceptable in conventional theory—would reduce, but not exclude, benefits. [62] A preference system à la Meade, on the other hand, is ideal from the point of view of conventional theory, in that tariff reductions are not carried further than the point where, on the margin, trade creation offsets trade diversion. This system, however, is not ideal from the point of view of the new customs-union theory.

However, even if trade diversion caused by preferences is not harmful and the welfare implications of preferences thus differ from those in conventional theory, there are risks that preferences, as opposed to the complete removal of obstacles to intratrade, will be ineffectual. The first reason why this may be so is the following: the trade barriers imposed before the formation of the preference area are likely to be so high, considering the difficulties in shutting out non-input imports from advanced countries, that partial de-restriction must be substantial for the arrangement to have any effect at all, whether in the form of trade creation or trade diversion. Otherwise, the trade obstacles still in force under the preferences might be fewer, but nonetheless prohibitive. For instance, the complete elimination of tariffs and quotas will have no effects as long as there are prohibitive exchange restrictions. The exchange arrangements in the most important existing integration scheme among developing countries, i.e., the Latin American Free Trade Association (LAF-TA), seem somewhat neglected. It might be important to emphasize that for economic integration among developing countries to have beneficial effects on balance of payments, there must not be, among the members, exchange restrictions ruling out an intensification of intratrade.

Second, there is a risk that preferences will not be operated in such a way as to give reasonable security to exporters who have succeeded, or might succeed, in entering the markets of other member countries. If, for instance, a preference is suddenly revoked in order to try to build up a domestic industry, this action—or the risk that it may take place—can cause considerable harm.

Finally, there is a third problem that, more than the first two, would assert itself in the intratrade relationships of developing countries: that of stimulating intratrade in a system of development planning.[63] To the extent that governments firmly commit themselves to national development plans, it will prove difficult to ensure a superior allocation of future additions to factors of production. Efforts should be made to avoid industrial duplications and the successive creation of new vested interests that, in combination with the original vested interests, may oppose a real freeing of intratrade. To this end, it is imperative to find a framework for the international coordination of development plans and to reach what could be called "agreed specialization."

This necessity has been well recognized in the developing countries. In the LAFTA treaty, there are provisions (Articles 16 and 17) for the negotiation of "complementary agreements."[64] The same is true of the General Treaty of Central American Economic Integration.[65] These questions have also received attention in Asia.[66] However, the area where the problems of regional cooperation at the planning stage seem to have been especially marked is Africa, with its fragmentation into small countries.[67] Although it is, as yet, perhaps too early for any practical results to have been achieved, it is an economic necessity in this region—and in Central America—to overcome nationalistic resistance to any relinquishment of complete sovereignty that might be involved in the coordination of development plans.

In view of the variety of noneconomic centrifugal forces, a complete customs union among developing countries might be considered too ambitious. It is therefore important to devise a policy framework that would minimize the risks of a preference arrangement's becoming void of significance. For this purpose, it could be suggested that the developing countries adopt a GATT code among themselves, at the same time that they pursue, to the extent that this is efficient, a more restrictive trade policy vis-à-vis the advanced countries. Within this "D-GATT," the member countries could achieve sufficient depth and discipline in their commitments. They could, for instance, decide not to apply quantitative restrictions among themselves and to negotiate tariff concessions or tariff bindings among themselves on a product-by-product or linear basis. The D-GATT could also serve the function of regulating the trade relationships among the various smaller customs unions of developing countries that might be formed.[68] To the D-GATT could also be tied a "D-PU" (Payments Union) to serve as a clearing institution for commercial payments. It could become a useful instrument, too, in the work on coordination of development plans; that is, it could serve as an International Planning Union.[69]

As to the advanced countries, they should not only accept this kind of trade policy, which in the language of conventional trade theory would amount to "discrimination," but even demand that the developing countries push ahead with integration schemes as ambitious as possible. Economic integration, even if only through preferences, does not constitute discrimination: the alternative to importing from another developing country is, on balance, not to import from an advanced country, but to try to produce the good domestically, if less efficiently. To minimize the support that advanced countries may have to give in order to bring about a certain rate of development—or, in other words, to maximize the return on a given development assistance program—they must show a marked interest in the economic integration of developing countries.

The Literature on Integration and Development

The literature on customs unions and underdeveloped countries is rapidly growing. One particular paper is of special interest, although it is concerned specifically neither with customs unions nor with underdeveloped countries. This is Fleming's paper on making the best of balance-of-payments restrictions.[70] Fleming assumes that a set of countries apply trade restrictions for balance-of-payments purposes. He then illustrates the effect of countries with a relatively strong balance of payments applying restrictions vis-à-vis relatively weak countries. These weaker countries will have to have more severe restrictions than would be necessary if the stronger ones had applied no restrictions against them. Such unnecessarily harsh restrictions would lead to welfare losses. Fleming defines the optimum structure of import restrictions as follows: if countries are arranged according to their balance-of-payments strength, a country should not apply any restrictions to weaker countries, although it may restrict imports from stronger countries. The country at the top should thus apply no restrictions at all and the one at the bottom would restrict imports from all countries.

As pointed out, Fleming *assumes* that the countries will operate balance-of-payments restrictions, in view of mounting political difficulities in using the conventional equilibrating mechanism. In this study, however, we have shown that it is *necessary* for developing countries to try to apply restrictions to relieve the effects of foreign-exchange gaps. If this important difference in background is disregarded, the Fleming optimum condition can be used to advocate exactly the trade policy outlined here. Let us divide countries into two distinct groups according to balance-of-payments strength; those without and those with foreign-exchange gaps, the former category including all the advanced countries. A further subdivision is not needed as long as it is assumed that countries with foreign-exchange gaps can equilibrate their intratrade accounts. Thus, there will be no hierarchy like the Fleming one, which was the result of his assumption that no countries would use conventional tools to achieve balance. But there will be two groups of countries with different balance of-payments strength, and as between these two groups the same conclusion applies. Countries with the same balance-of-payments strength should not apply trade obstacles among themselves but should pursue restrictions against the stronger countries without foreign-exchange gaps. Such an arrangement means, exactly, a customs union. Furthermore, to avoid additional deterioration of the weaker countries' balance of payments, the stronger countries without foreign-exchange gaps should not pursue any restrictions against them.

As to the literature specifically dealing with customs unions and underdeveloped countries, this is generally concerned with particular integration projects, the effects of which are scrutinized for normative, rather than for purely analytical, purposes. The conclusions reached on the central question, i.e., the effects of customs unions on growth, differ greatly. The sources of disagreement are principally of two different kinds. First, there is disagreement as to the *degree of implementation* of a particular project, in relation to what is understood, in theory, by a customs union. Second, there is disagreement as to the *effects* of the integration project, given the degree of implementation.[72]

Differences in opinion as to the degree of implementation amount to an institutional problem, on which the theoretical apparatus developed here does not shed any light. Instead, it is more interesting to study controversies over the effects of integration projects of a certain assumed degree of ambition and to compare these effects with the results reached here. Again, there are two principal sources of disagreement. The scope for economies of scale has been assessed differently, and the effects of changes in allocation have been viewed differently.

As to economies of scale, there is no dispute over the *direction* of the effects, these always being assumed to be positive as a result of an enlarged market. With regard to the *scope* for such economies, however, views differ greatly. But this is essentially an empirical question. The pivotal problem from a theoretical viewpoint is, instead, the treatment in the literature of the effects on allocation. There is sharp disagreement on this question. There are two different schools of thought, the distinguishing features of which make this conflict quite paradoxical. The first school, adhering to neoclassical trade theory, accepts neoclassical customs-union theory and takes a basically critical attitude toward customs unions among underdeveloped countries. The second school rejects neoclassical trade theory and neoclassical customs-union theory, taking a basically positive attitude toward customs unions among underdeveloped countries. This is paradoxical, because, as demonstrated in the present exposition, acceptance of the neoclassical trade theory ought to imply acceptance of customs unions among developing countries, whereas rejection of the neoclassical trade theory ought to rule out the acceptance of such customs unions. The solution of the paradox is, of course, that, to be able to accept customs unions among developing countries on the basis of a coherent theory, it is necessary both to accept and to reject the neoclassical trade theory. It must be rejected as an explanation of trade with advanced countries, but accepted as an explanation of trade with other developing countries. The first, conventional school is very explicit in its *full acceptance* of the neoclassical trade theory and thus reaches a negative conclusion, estimating the gains from trade creation to be smaller than the losses from trade diversion. On the other hand, the second school no more than *appears to be rejecting completely* the neoclassical theory but, although implicitly, actually accepts it as applicable to intratrade. In this way, the same conclusions as those advanced here have, in principle, been reached among the unorthodox writers.

The most forthright application of conventional customs-union theory to the problems of underdeveloped countries is that of R. L. Allen. Using familiar language, illustrated in the following quotations, he criticizes such customs unions.

> Trade creation, the basis for much of the confidence that the European Economic Community will prove economically sound, finds little prospect in less developed areas.[72]

> Import substitution resulting from added protection, however, cannot be regarded as an economic benefit resulting from integration. Indeed, in the short run, it may tend to misallocate resources even more than at present.[73]

> Some trade diversion will undoubtedly take place. Higher cost exports from other parts of the region would replace some of the present products imported from the outside.[74]

> The various proposals for integration make it abundantly clear that it is not the free trade ideal which is being pursued. They are all fundamentally protectionist, on a regional level, with respect to the exports of the industrialized countries, with the retention of sufficient protection on a national basis so that no real injury is inflicted. Such economic benefits as

might be expected from competition are specifically avoided by provisions insisted upon by those who might be damaged.[75]

Allen extends the logic of his argument to the problem of the allocation of future additions to resources. He points out that if the effects of reallocation are negative, it is likely that the future allocation will also be inferior, so that the customs union would reduce the dynamic efficiency.[76]

It is likely that a great number of economists hold views very similar to those advocated by Allen. This would not be surprising, for, as already underlined, such views follow from a straightforward application of that customs-union theory which most economists are likely to have accepted as being of general validity. But it is perhaps not to be expected that one will find many instances in the major theoretical journals, or similar sources of routine applications of standard customs-union theory to the case of underdeveloped countries.[77] After all, this would not represent any theoretical innovation. One application of conventional theory, made by Mikesell, is interesting from the present viewpoint in itself and also because of the fact that it produced an eloquent criticism by V. L. Urquidi, summing up the attitude of the unorthodox theorists toward the neoclassical trade and customs-union theory.[78] After a general sketch of the development problems, Urquidi notes that a customs union among developing countries serves the task of facilitating industrialization and that

> It is important to realize that the move toward the development of a free trade area under the Treaty of Montevideo was not inspired by the traditional theory of international trade and specialization and the resulting considerations about customs unions. The ultimate purpose is not to free intraregional trade as such, with whatever unhampered allocation of economic resources may result, but to reinforce mutually the process of economic development in the region. It should surprise no one that the framework provided for in the Treaty does not happen to fit a theoretical

free trade model, or correspond to the European Common Market procedures, or adapt itself literally to the provisions of GATT that were drafted thirteen years ago under quite different circumstances.[79]

Let us examine the constructive components of the alternative customs-union theory that has been suggested by those who, like Urquidi, have rejected the conventional theory. There are four sources which are of particularly great interest, one of which, interestingly enough, is a second and later paper by Mikesell. The other three are a report by the Economic Commission for Latin America (ECLA) and papers by R.S. Bhambri and H. Kitamura.[80] The only important difference among them is that Mikesell *assumes* that underdeveloped countries will indulge in import substitution, even if this is not necessarily the optimum policy,[81] while ECLA, Bhambri, and Kitamura treat import substitution as a *necessity*, in order to save foreign exchange for more important purposes than the importation of goods which could conceivably be produced domestically. In their chief argument for customs unions among underdeveloped countries, all four pursue the same approach. They see a customs union as a method of bringing about import substitution regionally, rather than domestically, in order to utilize the allocative advantages of international trade. Or, in the words of ECLA: "the establishment of a common market would have the advantage of enabling the (import) substitution process to be carried farther, without detriment to specialization possibilities, than would be possible within the sphere of each country's individual market."[82]

This approach also emphasizes economic integration as a framework for *future* allocation, rather than for present reallocation. Mikesell formulates this view in the following way:

> I believe, however, that the theoretical analysis of customs unions or of regional preference arrangements generally should be directed more towards the problem of their impact on the direction of investment in the developing countries for

future output rather than limited to an analysis of the welfare implications of shifting existing trade patterns. . . .
Very often there is relatively little trade among the members of regional trading blocs to begin with and virtually no
exports of manufactures either between members or to the
rest of the world. Hence, while the European Common Market
and the European Free Trade Area are striving to achieve an
expansion of intra-regional trade within the framework of an
existing economic structure, developing countries, such as
the members of the Latin American Free Trade Area, are
seeking to bring about within the next decade or two fundamental change in the structure of their production and trade
and have sought to fashion a regional trade mechanism which
will help to orient their economies in the direction of regional
specialization.[83]

Bhambri is the one who most clearly expresses the
implication of the import-substitution argument for the
conventional analysis of the welfare effects of trade diversion:

It is therefore reasonable to suggest that trade diversion
will be doubly beneficial. Firstly, by enlarging the size of
market for manufactures in both countries, increased trade
will help to reduce costs in industries where scale economies are important. Secondly, import substitution over a
wider area will enable the region as a whole to spend a
higher proportion of its foreign exchange on imports of capital goods and raw materials and help to increase the rate of
investment and economic growth.[84]

It is clear that there is close agreement between the
position of the unorthodox writers and the customs-union
theory suggested here. The only criticism that might be
made of the writings of those who have rejected the conventional theory of trade and customs unions is that their
analysis lacks a certain precision. But this is to be expected when a customs-union theory is not being deduced
from an explicit theory of trade in general. Basically, the
confusion arises when those writers, in refuting the conventional customs-union theory, reject the whole neo-

classical trade theory. However, this theory is needed to explain trade among developing countries and is, in fact, implicitly applied when advocating customs unions among underdeveloped countries. Thus, a theory that is explicitly rejected is implicitly used. Although most economists in advanced countries wish to apply conventional theory to the problems of underdeveloped countries, many economists in developing countries give the impression of not wanting to use that theory at all: both standpoints are equally fallacious. The quotation above from Urquidi might perhaps be considered as an illustration of too sweeping a rejection of conventional trade theory.[85]

This source of confusion will, hopefully, be avoided when we explicitly juxtapose the two sets of commercial policy conclusions that follow from, on the one hand, a new theory of trade with advanced countries, and, on the other hand, the neoclassical theory applied to trade among developing countries. One instance where this more systematic approach permits greater analytical precision relates to the distinction between the two different kinds of trade diversion, i.e., away from advanced countries and away from some other underdeveloped country. In spite of this criticism, however, it is noteworthy that the applied problem of customs unions among underdeveloped countries has stimulated many innovations in the theorizing on trade and development in general.

Conclusions

A number of conclusions emerge from the discussion of the commercial policies of developing countries. Points 1 to 9 below relate to trade policies vis-à-vis advanced countries, and Points 10 to 12 to trade policies among developing countries.

1. As commercial-policy interventions may be required to promote internal balance, there is a respectable case for antidepression protection. The intention, however, is not to reduce total imports but to restructure

them. Thus, the mechanics of this antidepression case for protection differs from the Keynesian one. This also means that these trade-policy measures cannot be classified as "beggar-my-neighbor" policies.

2. The restructuring of imports can, equally well, be considered as required from the balance-of-payments point of view. Looking at it from this angle, we are faced with a legitimate case for balance-of-payments restrictions, a case that, like antidepression protection, is only accepted as an inferior solution in conventional trade theory. As the restructuring of imports would aim, in particular, at abolishing luxury imports, we also have a case for a particular form of protection that has been rejected in the theory of trade policy.

3. Measures for restructuring imports and promoting exports must fulfil important efficiency criteria if they are to be acceptable. Owing to foreign-exchange difficulties, it is likely that all efficient projects cannot be effected at once. They should therefore be ranked according to the degree to which they save foreign exchange and be carried out in that order.

4. The case for infant-industry or infant-economy protection is somewhat less restrictive than in its usual version. This is due to the relaxation of the requirement that the infant industries eventually become internationally competitive. It is only required that the infant industries eventually become net savers of foreign exchange.

5. Exports should be stimulated up to the point where the earnings of foreign exchange, net of the import content in exports, are maximized, i.e., where the net marginal revenue of exports is zero.

6. Different theories of commercial policy apply to developing and advanced countries. There is a case for advanced countries nonreciprocally to free imports from developing countries. This will not only improve the terms of trade of the developing countries as part of economic aid, but will, in fact, promote the economic interest of the advanced countries themselves.

7. There is an optimum time path for the efficient

spending of stocks of foreign exchange in order to avoid wasteful construction of capacity, which, eventually, cannot be supplied with operation and reinvestment imports. There is therefore a special reason for holding foreign-exchange reserves in developing countries. The gains from holding certain reserves are larger than for advanced countries, but the costs of holding excess reserves are higher.

8. Capital imports requiring servicing may lead to a net loss in investment and income over time, unless they lead to an improvement in the foreign-exchange situation sufficient to pay for the servicing. This means that the developing countries might not be able to "afford capital imports."

9. The trade-policy situation of developing countries can be seriously aggravated by faulty expenditure policies, even if it cannot be completely rectified by optimum expenditure policies.

10. As to trade with other developing countries, a policy of nonrestricted trade should be pursued. To do this at the same time as restrictions are in force vis-à-vis imports from advanced countries, customs unions or other preferential arrangements should be established. One characteristic of the customs-union theory presented here is that trade diversion does not have negative effects so long as it is imports from advanced countries that are being diverted. Such trade diversion means that, thanks to the customs union, there has been a greater possibility of restructuring imports in favor of input imports. And the case for customs unions among developing countries is less indeterminate than for unions among advanced countries. (In the latter case, the static welfare gains could on balance be negative as well as positive.)

11. In order to implement unrestricted trade among developing countries, there must be a coordination of national development plans and attempts to reach "agreed specialization," in spite of the hampering effects on trade that detailed national planning may have. It is likely that national plans have to some extent been prompted by the

necessity to overcome the foreign-exchange difficulties
vis-à-vis the advanced countries—through a program of
import substitution, for instance.

12. In their trade relationships with backward countries, and possibly with backward regions in each country,
developing countries would have to adopt the same kind of
trade policies as those it has been suggested that advanced
countries pursue vis-à-vis developing countries.

IV

Backward Underdeveloped Countries: Trade and Trade Policy

We shall assume here that one distinguishing feature of backward countries or areas is the existence of obstacles to development efforts (insofar as there are such efforts), preventing these countries from making use of, or at least productive use of, expansion imports. The acquisition of expansion imports has no leverage effect on capacity growth, and the failure to obtain expansion imports leads to no frustration of additions to resources. There is also no need for reinvestment imports or imports of spare parts for operation purposes, these needs being derived from preceding imports of expansion inputs, but only for the primary-commodity component of operation imports. Since the size of such requirements depends upon the growth in preceding periods, even this import need too is unlikely to be important. Under all circumstances, the characteristic impact of trade on backward countries will not be assumed to derive from the effects of operation imports on capacity use.

This means that the theory of trade that has been formulated for the developing countries is not applicable to the conditions of backward countries or areas. For instance, under the conditions specified, the growth function in Figure 4 would coincide with the horizontal axis. Another theory—and another set of commercial policies—must be found.

A Theory of Trade

Trade affects backward countries through the changes in relative prices that occur when trade is opened up and conducted. In this, the impact is similar to that of trade

on advanced countries. But the neoclassical theory is
nonetheless inapplicable, for it assumes that changing
relative prices lead to a reallocation of factors of production, while in backward countries there will be no reallocation of factors.

The main welfare conclusions in neoclassical theory
can be upheld, however, as Haberler demonstrates, even
if it is assumed that factors of production are not reallocated. A country will nonetheless gain from trade
through a reallocation of consumption, effected via an
exchange on the international market of the given mix of
produced commodities. But there is one condition that
must be fulfilled: the factors engaged in the import-
competing sector must accept lower rewards. Otherwise,
the import-competing products will be unmarketable and
the factors of production unemployed. If such underutilization of capacity is great enough, the losses it entails
will more than offset the gains from a reallocation of
consumption.[1]

The argument that a reallocation of factors of production is not imperative for the realization of gains from
trade has been specifically applied to underdeveloped
countries—by Viner, for instance.[2] But it is interesting to
note that the factors of production in the import-competing sector may not be in a position to make what would
seem to be the rational choice, i.e., of preferring some
reduction in their rewards to unemployment. This is so
since factor wages in backward countries are usually so
low that they form part of subsistence incomes, which
ex definitione cannot be reduced.[3]

Thus, when analyzing the effects of shifts in relative
prices on backward countries, two basic changes are made
in the assumptions used in the analysis of effects on advanced countries. First, the factors of production are not
reallocated; second, there will not be full employment
when trade is opened up (assuming subsistence incomes).
The factors of production in the import-competing sector
are thus unable to defend themselves through either reallocation or reduction in their rewards.

Under these conditions, trade leads to completely different results from those set out in a conventional model. But before spelling out these results, it is necessary to ask whether a backward country necessarily has an import-competing sector, i.e., a sector in which the factors of production are defenseless when trade is being opened up. Let us look at the conventional two-country, two-commodity models, with both commodities being produced and consumed in both countries in the pretrade situation. There must necessarily—except in the special case when there is no difference in relative prices in the two countries—arise a diversion of demand away from one of the domestic sectors when trade is opened up. It is possible, however, to imagine circumstances in which there is no demand diversion: when the country in question in the pretrade situation does not produce any goods in the production of which it has a comparative disadvantage. There are two variants of this case: first, that a country actually produces only goods in which it has a comparative advantage; second, that a backward country in the pretrade situation produces only commodities which are not demanded abroad, and that only a vent-for-surplus commodity is offered on the world market when trade is opened up.[4] Then the export earnings represent net additions to demand and can be spent on imports without representing demand diversion. This second case might be of some practical interest, since the vent-for-surplus character of exports from a number of underdeveloped countries has been widely noted.[5]

If there is an import-competing sector, however, the effects of trade will differ greatly from those set out in the conventional analysis. The implications of a combined assumption of no reallocative capacity and subsistence incomes have been discussed elsewhere, and it is unnecessary to explore them in detail here,[6] but the effects of trade can be summarized in the following points:

1. Factors of production in the import-competing sector will first be left idle and then gradually be extinguished.[7]

2. The export sector will, as in conventional theory, benefit from an initial improvement in its terms of trade compared with the pretrade situation. There might also be some secular growth in the production potential of the export sector, without this contradicting the assumption of no reallocative capacity. Owing to such supply changes and to changes in foreign demand, the terms of trade of the export sector will change, up or down, through time. If the terms of trade deteriorate to the extent that incomes in the export sector are reduced below the subsistence level, this sector will be exposed to an extinction process, too.

3. Thus, trade has certain effects on capacity, although not through input imports, as in developing countries, but because an unfavorable price change has reduced productivity below the subsistence level. The fact that there will be changes in income and capacity, both in the import-competing sector (negative changes) and in the export sector (first positive changes, then, over time, positive *or* negative changes), means that a backward country is not necessarily a stationary economy.

4. Through the effects of trade on the export sector, this sector may eventually transform the economy, or part of it, into a developing economy. Yet it is also possible that the extinguished import-competing sector would have offered the best growth prospects.

Trade Policy

The strategic considerations that emerge from the theory just sketched and that must form the basis of a trade policy are: (1) whether there is an import-competing sector that would be extinguished and whether, in such a case, this could be avoided through some form of commercial-policy measures; (2) whether, even if there would be an extinction process, the gains accruing to the export sector would more than offset the losses; (3) whether the prospects for development improve or deteriorate through whatever structural changes are brought on by trade.

The possibility that a country can consider the effects of opening up trade without having to take into account the fortunes of an import-competing sector has already been commented on. The problem to which attention must presently be directed is rather whether it is possible to devise a commercial policy that permits a country to reap the export gains without the extinction of an import-competing sector. The only possible method to achieve this would be through some form of income transfer. Part of the exporters' gains would somehow have to be transferred to the factors in the import-competing sector, enabling these to reduce their rewards without falling below the subsistence-income level. This kind of income transfer would not be the same thing as conventional compensation, as discussed in welfare economics. The suggested compensation is intended not to ensure that a policy meets a certain welfare criterion, but, instead, to avoid various negative structural effects. Furthermore, the compensation must actually take place; it is thus not enough that it *could* be made. If such compensation is effected, extinction could be avoided and Haberler's main conclusion would hold. But it is highly questionable whether such compensation would be feasible in a backward country, on account of administrative problems.

Even if an extinction process cannot be avoided in the event that trade is opened up, this does *not* mean that if trade *has already been opened up*, the country should *close down* trade. Contrary to models where it is assumed that production factors can be reallocated and are fully employed, the process is not reversible in the model suggested here. If an import-competing sector has been extinguished through trade, it cannot be recreated through the mere closing down of trade.[8] Thus, the extinction of an import-competing sector should, once it has taken place, be regarded as a *sunk cost*. Evaluation of an optimum trade policy should then be based on other considerations relating to the export sector and growth prospects.

The gains of the export sector may or may not be
greater, the opening up of trade may or may not be advantageous (even if no compensation of the losers can take
place because of administrative obstacles), depending on
the welfare criterion applied and the effects of trade on
the growth prospects. It is also important to take into
account not only the immediate effects but also the future
development of the terms of trade. If the terms of trade
gradually improve, it is obvious that the opening up of
trade is a more attractive policy than it is if there is a
continuous deterioration.

Measures aiming at improving terms of trade thus play
a central part in the trade policy of backward countries.
Subsidies to the import-competing sector, intended primarily to prevent the extinction of this sector, could form
part of an optimum tariff policy. Measures to increase
foreign demand for exports should also be tried. The country may join a customs union in order to expand the market for its export (but it must secure the right to protect
the import-competing sector from extinction).

The question of customs unions is also relevant to the
effects of trade on prospects for development of a backward country. Basically, the question is whether the import-competing sector or export sector offers the best
growth prospects, a problem on which the theory outlined
here does not permit comment. But, if extinction of the
import-competing sector can be avoided, contact with foreign countries through trade would seem to increase the
possibility of becoming a developing country. Furthermore, in order to counter "polarization," there may be
certain investment agreements that aim not so much at
coordinated planning as at the distribution of benefits
within the customs union.[9] In actual practice, backward
countries have, in some instances, been accorded a priv-
ileged position in customs unions.

It is obvious from this short discussion that there is no
clear-cut answer to the question whether trade should be
opened up. It is, for instance, difficult, on the basis of
standard welfare criteria, to accept a policy that gives

rise to an extinction process, even if it leads to gains in the aggregate. Compensation tests are hardly applicable if the losers are extinguished. Furthermore, it may be found that growth prospects improve through the opening up of trade but that aggregate income is initially reduced. And the reverse conclusion may also be reached. Thus, there can be various conflicting elements entering into a final assessment. It might be noted, however, that the scope for such conflicts is very much reduced where the extinction of the import-competing sector need not be taken into account, trade already having been opened up. For such cases, the only conceivable policy is to continue trading and to try to create the best conceivable terms for the export industries. At the same time, it might be possible to become a developing country.

V

Concluding Comments

In this study, a distinction has been made between three country categories: advanced countries, developing countries with a foreign-exchange gap, and backward countries.[1]

Conventional trade theory has been applied to the advanced countries. The trade position of these countries has been discussed only to the extent that is found to be affected by the reconsideration of trade conditions in underdeveloped countries. The trade situation of backward countries has been touched on only briefly. Most of the attention has been directed to trade and trade policy in developing countries with a foreign-exchange gap. This reflects a recognition, first, that at least the most important underdeveloped countries belong to this category, in the sense that they have a developing sector or area holding out some promise for the future; and, second, that trade and trade policy have the most interesting role to perform in countries with acute foreign-exchange gaps.

Perhaps this discussion of trade problems of developing countries with foreign-exchange gaps can be criticized for exaggerating the role of trade and oversimplifying the development problems of such countries. But this study was not intended to be other than a treatise on trade theory, and, furthermore, not only is the theory of trade presented here a framework for the analysis of the effects of trade on growth, but other factors affecting development can be built into it. They enter into the analysis as factors influencing the shape and position, statically and dynamically, of the growth function in Figure 3. When discussing this function, it was emphasized that factors other than trade naturally affect the prospects of developing countries. In a sense, it can be argued that it is just through these other factors that trade in developing countries assumes the important role attributed to it. When these factors disappear, the country in question becomes an advanced country, and the role of trade is the one—and the less important one—set out in conventional trade theory. When, on the other hand, these factors are of even greater importance than in developing countries, the role of trade is also reduced—in this case to the status it assumes in backward countries.

It might also be argued that it is complicated to have a number of different trade theories applying to different kinds of countries. But there does not exist a more abstract, general theory of which the different trade theories outlined here could represent special cases. Conventional theory is no such general theory, and its presentation as such is, through its inability to explain certain salient facts, confusing.

Instead, a great many rival theories purport to explain the trade situation of underdeveloped countries. The present situation is, in fact, one of great confusion, uncertainty, and misunderstandings. For this reason, too, parallel trade theories suggested here represent a simplification, in that they permit a systematic interpretation and arrangement of various apparently conflicting views of trade and development.

Below, five different accounts of trade and development have been distinguished, and an attempt has been made to show how each of them fit into the analytical framework developed in this study.

1. *The conventional theory* applied to the case of underdeveloped countries by, for instance, Haberler and Viner.[2] Within the analytical framework of this study, the application of conventional theory is appropriate in the following cases: (a) Underdeveloped countries are likely to pursue suboptimal expenditure policies and thus aggravate their balance-of-payments problems, which are then handled through policies that lead to a suboptimal utilization of the production apparatus. (b) The intratrade problems of developing countries can, with proper modifi-

cations, having regard to the special conditions of trade
with advanced countries, be analyzed with the help of conventional trade theory. (c) If import-substitution and export-promotion policies in developing countries do not
satisfy the efficiency criteria, departures from a conventional trade policy would lead to a deterioration in the situation of a developing country. (d) It could be argued that
backward countries without an import-competing sector
would be affected by trade in the manner set out in conventional theory.

2. *The Nurkse-Seers theory.* Nurkse and Seers have
suggested that trade used to be an engine of growth but
that under present conditions it does not lead to a stimulation of growth, at least not to the same extent as before.[3] The explanation is said to be faltering demand in
the advanced countries for the primary products exported
by the underdeveloped countries. This view can be fitted
into the framework suggested here in the following ways:
(a) Backward countries face such development obstacles
that any stimulus derived from international trade peters
out. Some of the oil-producing countries, which Nurkse had
such difficulty in fitting into his analysis, probably belong
to this category. (b) Developing countries face a foreign-
exchange gap, whereas the former "areas of recent settle-
ments" were able either to earn more foreign exchange
in relation to their national income, or to satisfy their
needs for input imports at a lower relative level of
foreign-exchange earnings. For instance, consider the
"demonstration effect" on the capital-goods side, probably quite important in creating a psychological need to
base the development effort on the most modern—and imported—capital goods. The influence of this factor cannot
have been equally strong around the turn of the century as
it is today, when there is a greater economic distance between advanced and developing countries. The problem for
these developing countries is not whether the terms of
trade have improved or deteriorated, but that they are
not *sufficiently* favorable.

3. *The Myint theory.* Myint argues that underdeveloped

countries have experienced once-and-forall gains through trade and that trade has not induced a growth process.[4] The once-and-for-all gains might represent the gains that backward countries have experienced if they have not been exposed to the extinction of an import-competing sector— or if observers are unaware that such an extinction process has taken place.

4. The so-called *Prebisch-Singer-Myrdal thesis*, according to which underdeveloped countries have actually been hurt by international trade.[5] This case fits the case of backward countries that experience the extinction of an import-competing sector, particularly if this sector represented a better chance to transform the country into a developing economy.

5. The *Patel-Kitamura-Prebisch theory*, stating that the development effort of underdeveloped countries can only be fully realized through a great expansion of international trade.[6] This argument is, of course, synonymous with the position taken in the main part of this study. It should be noted, in this context, that it is not contradictory to argue, as Prebisch does, that trade is both bad and good for developing countries. It is bad in the sense that it has, *in fact*, not permitted the developing country to avoid frustration of part of its development effort; it is good in the sense that it *could* be turned into a super-engine of growth.

Notes

Preface

1. S. B. Linder, *An Essay On Trade and Transformation* (Göteborg and Uppsala and New York, 1961).

Chapter 1. Introduction

1. Excellent sources on the actual commercial policies of underdeveloped countries are the IMF *Yearbooks on Exchange Restrictions* and the GATT studies prepared for consultations with countries applying quantitative restrictions for balance-of-payments reasons. Unfortunately, however, the GATT papers have not been made public.

2. G. Haberler, *International Trade and Economic Development* (Cario, 1959), and J. Viner, *International Trade and Economic Development* (Oxford, 1953).

3. E. E. Hagen, "An Economic Justification of Protectionism," *Quarterly Journal of Economics*, LXXII (November, 1958), 496–514; R. E. Baldwin, "Exchange Rate Policy and Economic Development," *Economic Development and Cultural Change*, IX (July, 1961), 598–603. It should not be inferred that Hagen and others, by arguing that free trade is not an optimum policy, are implying that deviations from free trade in underdeveloped countries necessarily represent optimum policies.

4. The most outspoken and well-known writer in this group is R. Prebisch. See, e.g., his "Commercial Policy in the Underdeveloped Countries," *American Economic Review*, XLIX (May, 1959), 251–73, and the Report by the Secretary-General of the U.N. Conference on Trade and Development (Prebisch), published under the title *Towards a New Trade Policy for Development* (New York, 1964).

5. The relationship between static and dynamic efficiency is explored in R. Dorfman, P. A. Samuelson, and R. M. Solow, *Linear Programming and Economic Analysis* (New York, 1958), chap. xii. The implications of static efficiency for growth have hardly been applied to trade theory. A rudimentary attempt to do this can, however, be found in Linder, *op. cit.*, pp. 49–81. Within trade theory, changing factor totals and their effects have been discussed in some other contexts, too, namely (a) the effects of changes in factor prices on factor supply, both domestically and through international factor movements, and (b) the effects of exogenously determined growth on income through changing terms of trade.

None of these effects, however, represents an analysis of the central aspects of the effects of trade on growth.

6. Linder, *op. cit.*, chap. ii.

7. E.g., Haberler, "Some Problems in the Pure Theory of International Trade," *Economic Journal*, LX (June, 1950), 223–40.

8. See H. Kitamura, "Economic Theory and Regional Economic Integration of Asia," *The Pakistan Development Review*, II (Winter, 1962), 485–504; I. G. Patel, "Trade and Payments Policy for a Developing Country," in R. Harrod and D. C. Hague (eds.), *International Trade Theory in a Developing World* (London and New York, 1963); S. J. Patel, "Export Prospects and Economic Growth: India," *Economic Journal*, LXIX (September, 1959), 490–506; V. L. Urquidi, *Free Trade and Economic Integration in Latin America*, trans. M. M. Urquidi (Berkeley and Los Angeles, Calif., 1962); Prebisch, *op. cit.*, *Towards a New Trade Policy for Development*; H. Myint, "The 'Classical Theory' of International Trade and the Underdeveloped Countries," *Economic Journal*, LXVII (June, 1958), 317–37; R. Nurkse, *Patterns of Trade and Development* (Stockholm, 1959); and D. Seers, "A Model of Comparative Rates of Growth in the World Economy," *Economic Journal*, LXXII (March, 1962), 45–78.

Chapter 2. A Theory of Trade for Developing Countries

1. As noted in the Introduction, the effects of factor price changes on factor supply, domestically and through international factor movements, have been recognized. As the factor price changes are the result of reallocation, this represents the typical neoclassical extension of the theory in the direction of growth analysis. The effects on income growth of exogenously determined capacity growth through changes in terms of trade have also been analyzed.

2. It should also be noted that some statistical definitions of capital goods include some products which, in fact, serve consumption purposes. For instance, when capital goods are defined as SITC, Section 7 (machinery and transport equipment), passenger cars (Item 732.1) would be included, although in most cases they cannot be said to constitute input imports.

3. R. S. Eckaus, "Factor Proportions in Underdeveloped Areas," *American Economic Review*, XLV (September, 1955), 539–65.

4. For reasons to be explored further below, an escape from the need for balance cannot, except in special cases, be found in exports.

5. See pp. 114–22.

6. The formal possibility that part of the planned savings may not be frustrated because investments take the form of production for stock, e.g., of domestic capital goods that cannot be used unless combined with investment imports, is disregarded.

7. Since the discussion cannot be extended to cover various cyclical problems, it is assumed here that, in spite of the falling aggregate income, the desire to invest is not reduced.

8. To the extent that *ex-ante* savings are, by standard definitions, attempted savings, the planned savings here constitute a different category.

9. $M^+/\overline{Y} = p + ms_p$ is different from an ordinary propensity to import, although at first glance it might appear to be identical.

10. A line connecting those points on an underlying isoquant map that have the same marginal rate of substitution of factors of production.

11. As a matter of commercial policy, it may be appropriate under certain circumstances to encourage expansion imports even with some unfilled needs of maintenance imports. See chapter 3.

12. As a matter of commercial policy, this may be found advantageous. See chapter 3, pp. 92 and 96.

13. Similarly, it can be shown that, in Figure 2a, point P must be a stable equilibrium if there is a fixed volume of input imports. Domestic capacity will always adjust itself so that the fraction of operation imports is of such a magnitude that existing capacity can be fully used.

14. See chapter 3, p. 112.

15. In intrabloc trade, emphasis is on a search for optimum allocation of resources.

16. Criteria for trade and the planning of trade in centrally planned economies are discussed in a most interesting way by F. L. Pryor, *The Communist Foreign Trade System* (London and Cambridge, Mass., 1963), especially on pp. 55—63 and 100 ff. Another interesting account of the role of trade can be found in C. Bettelheim, *Studies in the Theory of Planning* (Bombay, 1959), from which the following pertinent characterization is taken (pp. 249—50):

> In relation to a planned national economy, external trade can play two distinct roles. On the one hand, it can *serve to fill in gaps—temporary or otherwise—between production and needs:* it can serve to meet deficits and get rid of surpluses resulting from a given plan and from the consumption that corresponds to it; to the extent that external trade limits itself to playing this role it fits into *the plan of a relatively autarkic economy.* On the other hand, external trade can *serve to bring about the specialisation of the country* in those kinds of production for which it is comparatively best suited; in this case, account must be taken of the influence of external trade when undertaking the actual planning of production; in other words, external trade then fits into the *plan of an economy which participates in the world-wide division of labour.* (Italics in original.)

17. The comparative-cost doctrine in the context of development economies has been surveyed by H. B. Chenery, "Comparative Advantage and Development Policy," *American Economic Review*, LI (March, 1961), 18—51; and J. Bhagwati, "The Theory of Comparative Advantage in the Context of Underdevelopment and Growth," *The Pakistan Development Review*, II (Autumn, 1962), 339—53.

18. Linder, *op. cit.*, pp. 82—109.

19. A report dated March 12, 1963, made at the request of the Board of Trade. A similar investigation, although broader in scope, has been made by the National Industrial Conference Board. See *The Conference Board Record*, I, No. 11 (November, 1964), 23—46.

20. In this context, it is instructive to remember Veblen's characterization of the needs for standardization to get a machine process to

function. "An unremitting requirement of quantitative precision, accuracy in point of time and sequence, in the proper inclusion and exclusion of forces affecting the outcome, in the magnitude of the various physical characteristics (weight, size, density, hardness, tensile strength, elasticity, temperature, chemical reaction, actinic sensitiveness, etc.) of the materials handled as well as of the applicances employed." *The Theory of Business Enterprise* (New York, 1904), p. 8.

21. The exact formula relating the elasticity of demand facing the particular country to the world elasticity of demand is

$$E = \frac{W + kR}{1 - k},$$

where E is the demand elasticity facing the country; W, the demand elasticity facing the world; R, the supply elasticity of the rest of the world; and k, the market share of the rest of the world. The rest of the world is assumed to pursue a price policy independent of the country. Since $(1 - k) \leq 1$ but ≥ 0, and $kR > 0$, $E > W$. The case $k \to lim\ 1$ is the case of infinite elasticity for individual producers $(E \to lim\ \infty)$ under free competition. If $k = 0$, and the individual country thus has 100 per cent of the market, $E = W$. The formula can be derived in the following way:

$$\frac{\frac{dq}{q}}{\frac{dp}{p}} = \frac{\frac{dq^w}{q^w}}{\frac{dp}{p}} \left(\frac{1}{1-k}\right) + \frac{\frac{dq^r}{q^r}}{\frac{dp}{p}} \left(\frac{k}{1-k}\right),$$

where w refers to the world and r to the rest of the world. The world demand elasticity

$$\frac{\frac{dq^w}{q^w}}{\frac{dp}{p}}$$

is calculated relating dq^w to q^w. However, from the point of view of the particular country, dq^w should be related to q, i.e., the amount sold at the original price by the particular country. If we multiply the world elasticity by the relation between the world quantity (1) and the quantity of the particular country $(1-k)$, we relate the world elasticity to the appropriate original quantity. If, e.g., the world elasticity = 2, and the share of the market of the particular country = 0.25 $(k = 0.75)$, then this component of the demand elasticity facing the particular country is four times as high, since the original quantity is four times smaller than the quantity used to calculate the value 2.

Similarly, the value for the supply elasticity of the rest of the world

$$\frac{\frac{dq^r}{q^r}}{\frac{dp}{p}}$$

cannot just be added to the value for the demand elasticity of the country, but must first be related to the appropriate quantity. This we do by multiplying by the second parenthesis. Depending upon whether the country has more or less than 50 per cent of the market, a smaller or bigger term than world supply elasticity will be added to the demand elasticity facing the particular country. The above expression is simplified into $E = W \ (1/1 - k) + R \ (k/1 - k)$ and can be written $E = W + kr/ 1 - k$, i.e., the formula first stated.

22. For a further discussion of this balance-of-payments concept, see F. Machlup, "Three Concepts of the Balance of Payments and the So-Called Dollar Shortage," *Economic Journal*, LX (March, 1950), 46–68.

23. As to the effects of exchange-rate changes, the implications of the foreign-exchange-gap analysis have been illustrated diagrammatically in the policy chapter. See pp. 80–82.

24. See, e.g. R. A Mundell, "The International Disequilibrium System," *Kyklos*, XIV (Fasc. 2, 1961), 153–72.

25. As to this concept, see M. Millikan and W. W. Rostow, *A Proposal: Key to an Effective Foreign Policy* (New York, 1957), chaps. vi and x; B. Higgins, *Economic Development* (New York, 1959), pp. 614–20; C. P. Kindleberger, *Economic Development* (New York, 1958), pp. 262–65; and R. F. Mikesell (ed.), *U. S. Private and Government Investment Abroad* (Eugene, Ore., 1962), chap. xiii.

26. U. N. Economic Commission for Latin America, *The Latin American Common Market* (New York, 1959), p. 71.

27. Government of India, Planning Commission, *Third Five Year Plan* (New Delhi, 1961), pp. 109–15.

28. Empirical material for such additional analyses of underdeveloped countries can be found in United Nations, *World Economic Survey, 1963* (New York, 1964), Part I, Table 3 A-1 and 3 A-2, p. 37.

29. GATT, *Trends in International Trade: A Report by a Panel of Experts* (G. Haberler, J. E. Meade, R. de Oliveira Campos, J. Tinbergen) (Geneva, October, 1958), p. 48.

30. *Ibid.*, p. 48.

31. *Ibid.*, p. 49.

32. The forceful renunciation of exchange controls by J. Marshall, "Exchange Controls and Economic Development," in H. S. Ellis and H. C. Wallich (eds.), *Economic Development for Latin America* (London and New York, 1961), pp. 430–51, is a good example.

33. From 109 in 1954 continuously to 100 in 1965, with 1958 as base year. See United Nations, *Statistical Yearbook, 1964* (New York, 1965), p. 496, and United Nations, *Monthly Bulletin of Statistics*, Special Table C, xx (March, 1966), xii.

34. See, for instance, S. J. Patel, *op. cit.*, pp. 490–506; U.N. Economic Commission for Latin America, *op. cit.*, pp. 53–83. See also various documents to the U. N. Conference on Trade and Development and the projections of the trade needs of underdeveloped countries that are reviewed below.

35. For instance, as pointed out to the author at a seminar in Mexico, Scotch whiskey in certain quantities is an input import into Mexico since it is needed in order to cater to American tourists.

36. The effectiveness of import controls is discussed at length in chapter 3.

37. Kitamura, *op. cit.*, p. 491.

38. Government of India, Planning Commission, *Third Five Year Plan*, p. 110.

39. D. T. Lakdawala, "Aspects of Trade Policy in India," *Indian Economic Journal*, XII (October-December, 1964), 89–110.

40. A. Waterston, "Development Planning: Lessons of Experience," to be published by Economic Development Institute of the International Bank for Reconstruction and Development; see chap. ix. The quotation from ECAFE is from *Economic Bulletin for Asia and the Far East*, XII (December, 1961), 12.

41. S. Dell, *Trade Blocs and Common Markets* (London, 1963), p. 170.

42. Situations in which certain maintenance imports should be eliminated in order to create room for expansion imports could be discerned. This is a matter of commercial policy; it is discussed in chapter 3, pp. 92–96.

43. United Nations, *World Economic Survey, 1962*, Part I (New York, 1963), pp. 5–9.

44. GATT, *International Trade, 1961* (Geneva, 1962), pp. 8–22.

45. B. Balassa, *Trade Prospects for Developing Countries* (Homewood, Ill., 1964).

46. *Ibid.*, p. 48.

47. R. Prebisch, who has approached the trade problems of underdeveloped countries in many different ways, is included in this group primarily because of views put forward in his Report to the U.N. Conference on Trade and Development. The appropriate references to W. A. Lewis, I. G. Patel, and V. L. Urquidi are as follows: Lewis, "Economic Development and World Trade" (mimeo from International Economic Association's meetings, Vienna, 1962); I. G. Patel, "Trade and Payments Policy for a Developing Economy," in Harrod and Hague (eds.), *op. cit.*, pp. 309–31; and Urquidi, *op. cit.*

48. I. G. Patel, *op. cit.*, pp. 310–11. From the paper by S. J. Patel which has already been quoted ("Export Prospects and Economic Growth: India"), the passages below may be cited as additional illustrations:

> The lagging behind of output in the export sector would not be a matter for much concern as long as the rate of growth of output in the other sectors of the economy could be raised sufficiently to offset the slow development in the export sector. It is in this field, however, that developments in the export trade can be expected to exercise a decisive influence on the growth of the Indian economy by affecting the volume and the rate of expansion of import capacity. Since India depends on imported capital equipment for more than half of the total equipment used in investments in the country, the slow expansion in export proceeds, and hence import capacity, places a serious limitation upon increasing the imports of capital-goods. The volume and the rates of growth of investment, and therefore real income, in the country are thus inhibited. (P. 502).
> Since, under the present international division of labour, capital-

goods are almost exclusively imported from the industrial countries, expanding the supplies of these goods means that import capacity (i.e., export proceeds) has to increase correspondingly. The growth of import capacity, however, is dependent not upon the need for enlarging the supplies of capital-goods for development but upon the import demand of the industrial countries, which has in general tended to grow at a rate lower than the real product in industrial countries. Thus the needs of capital-goods imports outrun by far the supply potential of capital-goods as a result of the much slower growth of import capacity.

Consequently, whenever a pre-industrial country embarks upon a determined drive to expand investments, it is soon faced with a serious balance-of-payments crisis. The pace falters, the drive slackens and the will evaporates in a frustrating stagnation. (P. 503).

It might be added here that, although the writings of Bhagwati are not typical of this approach, he has, in a short passage, observed the possibility that there might be a zero rate of transformation of domestic resources into capital goods through production and that, owing to diminishing returns, there might be a rapidly falling rate of transformation through exports. In such a case, one would have to distinguish between a limit to investment set by the capacity to save goods for export and by the possibility of converting export goods into export earnings. See Bhagwati, "Indian Balance of Payments Policy and Exchange Auctions," *Oxford Economic Papers*, N. S., XIV (February, 1962), 55–56.

49. A. O. Hirschman, *The Strategy of Economic Development* (New Haven, 1958), p. 166. J. Tinbergen might be mentioned among other economists whose principal background has been concerned with advanced countries and who have expressed similar views. See his *The Design of Development* (Baltimore, 1958), pp. 39–40: "In a number of countries there is, in addition, a fundamental disequilibrium in the balance of payments only too well-known, and which it would be rash to ascribe to financial mismanagement only."

The following comment by Little on a book by Reddaway might also be of interest: See I. M. D. Little, review of W. B. Reddaway's *The Development of the Indian Economy*, in *Economic Journal*, LXXII (September, 1962), 722–23.

Mr. Reddaway accepts a general view of the Indian economy which is, I believe, not only common to all or almost all those economists who have been at all closely concerned with Indian Planning but is also the official view. If India is to develop at the minimum rate (say 5%) which seems to be politically and humanistically reasonable in the light of her $2\frac{1}{2}$% rate of population growth, there will inevitably be a large increase in demand for the kind of things at present she mainly imports—industrial materials and machinery. There is absolutely no chance, whatever internal policies are pursued, of expanding her foreign-exchange earnings enough to meet the rapidly rising import bill. ... Hence also the fact that there is a balance-of-payments case for India, which is *not* merely a reflection of inadequate domestic savings.

50. Hirschman, *op. cit.*, pp. 166–73. The quotation is from p. 172 (italics in original). It should also be pointed out that the concept of "frustration" of additions to domestic resources, a concept used in this study, is taken over from Hirschman, who argues, in general, that investment in underdeveloped countries is often held back not by a lack of savings but by a lack of investment opportunities and that domestic savings might be "frustrated." Presumably, to judge from the reasoning reviewed in the text above, one reason for a lack of investment opportunities could be lack of imported inputs to use in the *R*-sector.

51. A. S. Manne, "Key Sectors of the Mexican Economy, 1960–70," in A. S. Manne and H. M. Markowitz (eds.), *Studies in Process Analysis* (New York, 1963). See also, for the same approach, H. B. Chenery and M. Bruno, "Development Alternatives in an Open Economy: The Case of Israel," *Economic Journal*, LXXII (March, 1962), 79–103; R. I. McKinnon, "Foreign Exchange Constraints in Economic Development and Efficient Aid Allocation," *Economic Journal*, LXXIV (June, 1964), 388–409; Tinbergen, *op. cit.*, especially pp. 39–40, and, by the same author, "Spardefizit und Handelsdefizit," *Weltwirtschaftliches Archiv*, XCV (January, 1965), 89–99; and R. F. Mikesell, *Public Foreign Capital for Private Enterprise in Developing Countries* (Princeton Essays in International Finance, No. 52) (Princeton, N.J., 1966).

Chapter 3. Trade Policy for Developing Countries

1. See, e.g., H. G. Johnson, "Optimum Tariffs and Retaliation," *Review of Economic Studies*, XXI (1953–54), 142–53; and *International Trade and Economic Growth* (Cambridge, Mass., 1958).

2. If the propensity to save is high in a country applying an optimum tariff and low in other countries, world savings might increase in spite of the fall in world income.

3. See, e.g., Hagen, *op. cit.* For a criticism of Hagen's originally overstated case, see, e.g., P. B. Kenen, "Development, Mobility and the Case for Tariffs: A Dissenting Note," *Kyklos*, XVI (Fasc. 2, 1963), 321–24.

4. If a learning period results in economies *internal* to the firm, there need not be any infant-industry protection, since the initial losses, like any other investment outlays, should be possible to recoup. (The only difficulty would be the lack of opportunities in an underdeveloped country to finance such immaterial investments on an imperfect capital market or through self-finance.) If the economies are *external* to the firm, however, today's prices will leave no room for yesterday's losses. Training is regularly thought to be the most important source of external economies. However, the question arises whether, through a reduction in wages, the trainees, rather than the firm, will carry the training costs. Empirical research by G. S. Becker suggests that this is the case, as soon as the training is "general," i.e., can be used outside the firm providing the training facilities. See Becker, "Investment in Human Capital: A Theoretical Analysis," *The Journal of Political Economy*, LXX (October, 1962), Supplement, 9–49. In underdeveloped countries, trainees may, however, find themselves in a position where they cannot finance their training, either through a wage reduction or

through borrowing. Then, if the government does not provide training facilities itself or through a direct subsidy, there must be indirect subsidization through protection during the learning period. For further comments on the infant-industry argument, see below, pp. 93-94.

5. As to negative effects of "beggar-my-neighbor" policies, see, e.g., R. Nurkse, "Domestic and International Equilibrium," in S. E. Harris (ed.), *The New Economics: Keynes' Influence on Theory and Public Policy* (New York, 1947), pp. 264–92. With regard to the fallacy of balance-of-payments controls, see, e.g., J. E. Meade, *The Theory of International Economic Policy*, Vol. I: *The Balance of Payments* (London and New York, 1951), p. 318.

6. See Meade, *op. cit.*, p. 318:

> It is often argued that the authorities in a deficit country should not permit the waste of scarce foreign currency on luxuries. It is claimed that the import of necessities (e.g., wheat) should be permitted and that of luxuries (e.g., motor-cars) disallowed. But this is quite erroneous. The standard of living in a deficit country will have to be reduced when the deficit on its balance of payments is removed, since its domestic expenditure will have to be reduced to maintain internal balance as its imports decrease and exports increase; and it may well be that when its standard of living is reduced, its residents should give up consuming motor-cars (whether imported or home-produced) and should go on consuming wheat. But, if, when the balance of payments is once again in balance, motor-cars as well as wheat are still being consumed there is no more reason why wheat should be imported and motor-cars made at home than vice versa.

7. For instance, Haberler writes that "the burden of proof is on those who maintain that the exceptions (instances where private money costs do not reflect social real costs) are numerous, persistent, large, and, last but not least, practically recognizable and calculable." Haberler, "Some Problems in the Pure Theory of International Trade," p. 238.

8. A. C. Harberger, "Using Resources at Hand More Effectively," *American Economic Review*, XLIX (May, 1959), 134–46.

9. These countries would be best served by conventional commercial policies with due modifications.

10. For the derivation of supply and demand curves of foreign exchange, see, e.g., A. G. Hart and P. B. Kenen, *Money, Debt, and Economic Activity* (3d ed.; Englewood Cliffs, N.J., 1961), pp. 313 ff. Supply curves of foreign exchange will have the particular shape of the curve in Figure 4 for the following reasons: at some very low price for foreign currency in terms of the currency of the developing country, foreigners will not buy any goods at all of the export products of the developing country, as these are prohibitively expensive. This intercept with the y-axis corresponds to the point on the underlying foreign-demand curve for exports of the developing country where, owing to a high price, demand is zero. The supply of foreign exchange will reach a maximum where foreign demand for exports from the developing country times the price of these exports in foreign currency reaches a maximum, i.e.,

where the foreign-demand curve for exports from the developing country
has unitary elasticity. If the price of exports from the developing country is lowered, i.e., the currency of the developing country devalued,
meaning a movement upward on the y-axis in Figure 4, the developing
country will sell more commodities, but at so much lower a price that
the foreign-exchange earnings of the developing country will diminish.
Thus, the supply curve of foreign exchange becomes backward sloping.
It will approach the y-axis asymptotically as the currency is devalued
more and more, since only when the currency is infinitely devalued
could the curve intersect the y-axis.

11. *Ibid.*, pp. 316–18.

12. It might be argued that the quantity of required input imports
would vary with the amount of exports produced, which is a function of
the exchange rate. However, the relative size of the exports, apart
from influencing how much could *actually* be imported, will only determine the amounts of input imports required in the export sector. To
the extent that this falls, there will be a corresponding rise in the input-
import requirement in other sectors to maintain internal balance. Total
input imports will be unaffected. If, on the other hand, the assumption
of internal balance is dropped, the demand curve would be elastic.

13. Pryor, *op. cit.*, pp. 28–29.

14. Alternative commercial policy measures are discussed in, for
instance, C. P. Kindleberger, *International Economics* (3d ed.; Home-
wood, Ill., 1963), Part III; League of Nations (Haberler), *Quantitative
Trade Controls* (Geneva, 1943); Meade, *op. cit.*, Part V; and E. R.
Schlesinger, *Multiple Exchange Rates and Economic Development*
(Princeton Studies in International Finance, Vol. II) (Princeton, N.J.,
1952); A. Kafka, "The Brazilian Exchange Auction System," *Review of
Economics and Statistics*, XXXVIII, (August, 1956), 308–22; Bhagwati,
"Indian Balance of Payments Policy and Exchange Auctions," pp. 51–
68; E. M. Bernstein, "Some Economic Aspects of Multiple Exchange
Rates," *International Monetary Fund Staff Papers*, I (1950–51), 224–37;
and "Mudaliar Report," Government of India, Ministry of Commerce
and Industry, *Report of the Import and Export Policy Committee* (New
Delhi, 1962).

15. The restrictions could take the form of tariffs, quantitative restrictions, multiple exchange rates, and/or direct exchange controls.

16. M. F. W. Hemming and W. M. Corden use the expression "partial equilibrium approach" to distinguish between a crude theory of the
balance-of-payments effects of import restrictions and more refined
versions. See their "Import Restriction as an Instrument of Balance-
of-Payments Policy," *Economic Journal*, LXVIII (September, 1958),
483–510.

17. A special case of this possibility is that the government saves
some tariff proceeds.

18. These arguments *pro et contra* are advanced by Hemming and
Cordon, *op. cit.*, p. 484. Bhagwati agrees with the negative assessment
of the savings effect, "Indian Balance of Payments and Exchange Auctions," p. 60.

19. *Ibid.*

20. The evasion of controls may be quite an important factor. It is,

of course, difficult to obtain any statistical information on the losses of foreign exchange in these ways. However, in his study of the Philippines, F. H. Golay concludes: "On the basis of the available evidence it seems clear that illegal and legal transactions in evasion of exchange controls amount to at least one-quarter, and are probably equal to one-third of the export proceeds currently channeled to the Central Bank." It should also be noted that controls may be evaded even in the case where there is unused capacity in the economy. See Golay, *The Philippines: Public Policy and National Economic Development* (Ithaca, N.Y., 1961), p. 161.

21. There is a third, strategic difference, which has already been stressed several times. This is that advanced countries fulfilling the precondition, unlike the developing countries, still do not have a good case for using this method to establish external equilibrium.

22. The fraction p here is identical to the fraction p used when discussing the implications of the factor-proportions problem.

23. Nurkse, *Patterns of Trade and Development*, p. 36.

24. As to the definition of the infant-industry case in conventional theory, see p. 76.

25. This is what Kemp refers to as the "Bastable criterion." See M. C. Kemp, "The Mill-Bastable Infant-Industry Dogma," *Journal of Political Economy*, LXVIII (February, 1960), 65–67.

26. H. Myint, "Infant Industry Arguments for Assistance to Industries in the Setting of Dynamic Trade Theory," in Harrod and Hague (eds.), *op. cit.*, p. 175.

27. Note that this hierarchy of projects must then be related to the hierarchy of export-promoting projects.

28. These measures may consist of subsidies, production taxes, export quotas, currency-retention schemes, multiple exchange rates, etc.

29. An interesting way in which, in actual practice, a nonobservation of the efficiency criterion has resulted in negative value added and foreign-exchange losses is pointed out by Bernstein, *op. cit.*, 229–30. He notes that multiple exchange rates have in some instances been so constructed that a manufacturer has been able to make a profit in domestic currency by importing some raw materials or semimanufactures at a low exchange rate; exposing these to some token processing, and then exporting them at a high exchange rate, but actually receiving a lower price in foreign currency than that paid for the input imports.

30. If the advanced countries would, in fact, improve their payoff through some restrictions, this would be a case in which a country or country group (i.e., in this case, the advanced countries) would gain from optimum tariffs in spite of retaliation; although, of course, the tariffs applied by the developing countries cannot be looked upon as retaliation in search of an optimum tariff in the conventional sense. For an answer to the question of why developing countries are not trying to formulate optimum tariffs of the conventional kind, see p. 99.

31. The subsequent analysis draws heavily on a study the author has made for the U. N. Conference on Trade and Development. See Linder, "The Significance of GATT for Under-Developed Countries" (U.N. Doc. E/CONF. 46/P/6) (mimeo; Geneva, January, 1964). For other sources on the problem of GATT and developing countries, see U.N. Conference

on Trade and Development, "The Developing Countries in GATT" (U.N. Doc. E/CONF. 46/36) (mimeo; Geneva, March, 1964); "The Role of GATT in Relation to Trade and Development," a paper contributed by the GATT Secretariat (U.N. Doc. E/CONF. 46/38) (mimeo; Geneva, March, 1964); J. Royer, *In Defence of GATT* (London, 1963); and I. Gal-Edd, *The General Agreement on Tariffs and Trade and the Developing Nations* (Israel, 1961).

32. Surprisingly enough, underdeveloped countries have made little use of the special provision made for alleviation of their obligations (Art. XVIII A and C); but this is primarily because it has proved so easy to defend the application of even virtually permanent quantitative restrictions for balance-of-payments purposes (Art. XVIII B).

33. Uruguay has complained that her exports are subject to a great number of protectionist measures not permitted under the trade rules embodied in GATT. The complaints have been backed up by extensive lists of such illegal measures. See GATT, *Basic Instruments and Selected Documents, Eleventh Supplement* (Geneva, March, 1963).

34. Geneva, 1947, 1956, and 1960−61; Annecy, 1949; and Torquay, 1951−52.

35. If Israel is excluded from the category of underdeveloped countries, the figure 39 is reduced to 28.

36. These data are from the author's U.N. study, *The Significance of GATT for Under-Developed Countries*, pp. 13 ff.

37. Such trade obstacles are surveyed in United Nations, *World Economic Survey, 1962*, Part I, pp. 31−40 and 65−70. For a discussion of these trade obstacles, see also Dell, *op. cit.*, chap. v.

38. P. K. Bardhan, "Investment Pattern and the External Balance," *The Economic Weekly* (India), XIV (July, 1962), 1207.

39. A description of the relatively unknown device of "compensatory financing" can be found in, e.g., United Nations, *World Economic Survey, 1962*, Part I, pp. 55−58. To avoid confusion, the term "compensatory financing" used in this sense of reimbursing developing countries for a deterioration in raw material prices must be distinguished from the original, and more general, sense in which the concept of compensatory financing has been used—i.e., to separate those items in the accounting balance of payments that have the character of balancing the autonomous items. In the original sense, "compensatory finance" is thus synonymous with "accommodating finance" (and "induced finance"). Compensatory financing in the new sense is a form in which compensatory financing in the latter, original sense can take place. This relationship, in fact, explains how the one sense has developed out of the other.

40. Although it is slightly inadequate from a balance-of-payments accounting point of view, donations are treated as a capital-account item.

41. There are some doubts as to the benefits of farm-surplus disposal. For evidence of negative price effects, see, e.g., Dell, *op. cit.*, pp. 138−39. The possibility of negative effects on domestic agricultural production has been discussed by, among others, T. W. Schultz, "Value of U.S. Farm Surplus to Underdeveloped Countries," *Journal of Farm Economics*, XLII (December, 1960), pp. 1019−30; D. R. Khatkhate,

"Some Notes on the Real Effects of Foreign Surplus Disposal in Underdeveloped Countries' Economies," *Quarterly Journal of Economics*, LXXVI (May, 1962), 186–96, with comments by C. Beringer and W. F. Falcon in *Quarterly Journal of Economics*, LXXVII (May, 1963), 317–26.

42. M. Friedman, "The Case for Flexible Exchange Rates," in his *Essays in Positive Economics* (Chicago, 1953), pp. 182–87.

43. See B. F. Massel, "Export Concentration and Fluctuations in Export Earnings: A Cross-Section Analysis," *American Economic Review*, LIV (March, 1964), 47–63.

44. Capital transactions in the form of the reception of aid and the running down of international excess assets cannot lead to a widening of the foreign-exchange gap.

45. See Kindleberger, *International Economics*, pp. 393–94; W. R. Allen, "Domestic Investment, the Foreign Trade Balance, and the World Bank," *Kyklos* XV (Fasc. 2, 1962), 353–73; Higgins, *op. cit.*, pp. 625–26.

46. See G. C. Woods's speech at the IBRD Annual Meeting in the fall of 1963, reprinted in *International Financial News Survey*, XV (October 4, 1963), 338–42.

47. Kindleberger in *International Economics*, pp. 400–401, argues that "the notion that a country must borrow to pay interest on old loans is nonsense. Old loans pay their own way through increased productivity *and* the transformation of the economy which shifts resources among sectors." In our framework, however, it is not nonsense to speak of borrowing to service, since old loans do not necessarily pay their "foreign-exchange way."

48. See p. 1 of the first IBRD report to UNCTAD, referred to in footnote 49 below.

49. In chronological order, the following works might be cited: G. M. Alter, "The Servicing of Foreign Capital Inflows by Under-Developed Countries," originally prepared in 1953, read at the IEA Rio Round Table Conference in 1957, and published in 1961 in Ellis and Wallich (eds.), *op. cit.*; D. Avramovic, *Debt Servicing Capacity and Postwar Growth in International Indebtedness* (Baltimore, 1958; D. Avramovic and R. Gulhati, *Debt Servicing Problems of Low-Income Countries*, 1956–1958 (Baltimore, 1960); Mikesell, "The Capacity to Service Foreign Investments," in Mikesell (ed.), *op. cit.*; "Economic Growth and External Debt--An Analytical Framework," a report prepared by IBRD for the U.N. Conference on Trade and Development (U.N. Doc. E/CONF. 46/84) (mimeo; Geneva, March, 1964). For historical data on foreign-debt-servicing, see, e.g., D. Finch, "Investment Service of Underdeveloped Countries," *International Monetary Fund Staff Papers*, II (September, 1951), 60–85; and "Economic Growth and External Debt-- A Statistical Presentation," another report prepared by IBRD for UNCTAD (U.N. Doc. E/CONF. 46/40) (mimeo; Geneva, March, 1964).

50. Alter, *op. cit.*, p. 141.

51. IBRD, *Economic Growth and External Debt--An Analytical Framework*.

52. *Ibid.*, p. 8.

53. *Ibid.*, pp. 22–24.

54. *Ibid.*, pp. 24–25.

55. *Ibid.*, p. 41.

168   *Notes*

56. *Ibid.*, p. 35.

57. Vis-à-vis backward countries, there might have to be a unilateral abolishment of trade obstacles or some special treatment for
these countries. These questions are discussed in chapter 4.

58. The literature setting out the implications of conventional trade
theory on the problem of customs unions is abundant. The following
works can be consulted for original contributions and summaries. J.
Viner, *The Customs Union Issue* (New York, 1950); J. E. Meade, *The
Theory of Customs Unions* (Amsterdam, 1955); R. O. Lipsey, "The
Theory of Customs Unions: A General Survey," *Economic Journal*, LXX
(September, 1960), 496–513; B. Balassa, *The Theory of Economic Inte-
gration* (Homewood, Ill., 1961).

59. However, trade creation may save foreign exchange, too, through
lower total input-import requirements to produce the volume of goods
originally produced in each country in isolation.

60. See, e. g., Balassa, *The Theory of Economic Integration*, pp.
29–49.

61. Meade, *The Theory of Customs Unions*, pp. 110–14. Referring
to effects of trade other than those of allocation, the Meade argument
has been criticized by Mikesell, "The Theory of Common Markets as
Applied to Regional Arrangements among Developing Countries," in
Harrod and Hague (eds.), *op. cit.*, pp. 213–15.

62. The fact that selective preferences can be shown not to be harmful means that integration of only certain productive sectors of developing
countries (as with the European Coal and Steel Community) is acceptable.

63. As to the difficulties of utilizing the advantages of allocation
through trade under a system of national planning, it is interesting to
consult Pryor, *op. cit.*, pp. 35–37, 199–224, and 260–66.

64. See, for instance, Prebisch, *Towards a Dynamic Development
Policy for Latin America*, pp. 94–98.

65. U.N. Economic Commission for Latin America, "General Situation and Future Outlook of the Central American Integration Programme," (U.N. Document E/CN. 12/666) (mimeo; Mar del Plata, May,
1963).

66. See, for instance, D. T. Lakdawala, "Trade Cooperation Within
the ECAFE Region," *The Pakistan Development Review*, II (Winter,
1962), 505–42.

67. See "Co-ordination of Development Plans in Africa," *Economic
Bulletin for Africa*, IV, No. 1, Part B (January, 1964), 1–69; the U.N.
Economic Commission for Africa's Reports of the three Industrial Co-
ordination Missions (to West Africa, North Africa, and East and Central
Africa, respectively) (U.N. Doc. E/CN. 14/246–48) (mimeo; Addis
Ababa, 1964).

68. It could also lay down the principles of trade policy vis-à-vis
backward countries (to be discussed in the subsequent chapter) and
press for concessions from advanced countries (discussed in chapter 3).

69. The various institutional functions and requisites for economic
integration among developing countries are discussed in an interesting
way by M. S. Wionczek in the introductory chapter to Wionczek (ed.),
Latin American Economic Integration: Experiences and Prospects (New
York, 1966).

70. M. Fleming, "On Making the Best of Balance of Payments Restrictions on Imports," *Economic Journal*, LXI (March, 1951), 48–71.

71. The literature on underdeveloped countries and economic integration includes, *inter alia*, the following works: R. L. Allen, "Integration in Less Developed Areas," *Kyklos*, XIV (Fasc. 3, 1961), 315–36; Balassa, *The Theory of Economic Integration*, pp. 53–56, 118–19, 138–43, and 161–62; R. S. Bhambri, "Customs Unions and Underdeveloped Countries," *Economía Internazionale*, XV (May, 1962), 235–58; Dell, *op. cit.*, chaps. v–vii; Federal Reserve Bank of New York, "The Emerging Common Markets in Latin America," *Monthly Review*, XLII (September, 1960), 154–60; R. Harrod, "Economic Development and Asian Regional Cooperation," *The Pakistan Development Review*, II (Spring, 1962), 1–22; Kitamura, "Economic Theory and Regional Economic Integration of Asia"; B. F. Massell, "East African Economic Union: An Evaluation and Some Implications for Policy" (Rand Corporation Memorandum (mimeo; Santa Monica, Calif., December, 1963); R. F. Mikesell, "The Movement Toward Regional Trading Groups in Latin America," in Hirschman (ed.), *Latin American Issues: Essays and Comments* (New York, 1961), pp. 125–51; Mikesell, "The Theory of Common Markets as Applied to Regional Arrangements Among Developing Countries," pp. 205–29; Prebisch, *Towards a Dynamic Development Policy for Latin America*, pp. 89–103; U.N. Economic Commission for Latin America, *The Latin American Common Market* (New York, 1959); V. L. Urquidi, "The Common Market as a Tool of Latin America's Economic Development: A Comment," in Hirschman (ed.), *op. cit.*, pp. 151–60; Urquidi, *Free Trade and Economic Integration in Latin America*; R. Vernon, "A Trade Policy for the 1960's," *Foreign Affairs*, XXXIX (April, 1961), 458–70; Wionczek, "The Montevideo Treaty and Latin American Economic Integration," *Banca Nazionale del Lavoro Quarterly Review*, LVII (June, 1961), 197–240; the contributions by Wionczek, Balassa, Kitamura, and Linder in Wionczek (ed.), *op. cit.*

72. Allen, *op. cit.*, p. 330.

73. *Ibid.*, p. 331.

74. *Ibid.*

75. *Ibid.*, p. 332.

76. *Ibid.*, pp. 332–34.

77. Harrod in the following quotation has had particular occasion to repeat the standard argument in "Economic Development and Asian Regional Cooperation," pp. 11–12.

In the case of the Asian region, there did not seem to be much scope for trade "creation," since much production was governed by the pattern of natural resources, while manufacturing industry was in its early stage, and the scope for eliminating high-cost manufacturers within the region was, therefore, not great. On the other hand, there might be a considerable amount of trade "diversion," *viz.*, replacement of high-cost production within the region for low-cost production outside it. This would be uneconomical and wasteful. And, as explained above, the developing countries can ill afford to waste.

This comment is from a summary of the proceedings at a round table of Asian economists. Since at least some of the papers read at that conference (for instance, the Kitamura one that is reviewed below) seem to take a very different attitude, the Harrod conclusions are perhaps to some extent prompted by a wish to offer what he considers to be a superior theoretical interpretation of the effects of integration among the underdeveloped countries of Asia, i.e., an assessment in terms of conventional theory.

78. Both these contributions are from Hirschman (ed.), *op. cit.*

79. Urquidi, in Hirschman (ed.), op. cit., pp. 155–56.

80. The ECLA Report referred to is *The Latin American Common Market;* Mikesell, "The Theory of Common Markets as Applied to Regional Arrangements Among Developing Countries; Bhambri, *op. cit.* ; Kitamura, "Economic Theory and Regional Economic Integration of Asia."

81. Thus, the Mikesell paper can be said to be a direct application of the Fleming criterion on making the best of balance-of-payments restrictions.

82. ECLA, *The Latin American Common Market*, p. 67.

83. Mikesell, "The Theory of Common Markets as Applied to Regional Arrangements Among Developing Countries," p. 206.

84. Bhambri, *op. cit.*, p. 245.

85. See above, pp. 136–37.

Chapter 4. Backward Underdeveloped Countries: Trade and Trade Policy

1. See Haberler, "Some Problems in the Pure Theory of International Trade."

2. See Viner, *International Trade and Economic Development*, pp. 37–38.

3. If the assumption of subsistence incomes is modified and allowance is made for a separate class of landowners and capitalists with incomes above subsistence, there is room for some reduction in factor rewards. Then, the negative effects can be avoided under the double assumption that (1) the factor owners who obtain lower rewards do not reduce the supply of their factors, thereby reducing the physical productivity of the factor with subsistence incomes (labor); and (2) this latter factor category (labor) does not consume any other product than the import-competing good, so that the change in price ratios does not affect its real income. This case has been pointed out by Kenen in his review of Linder, *An Essay on Trade and Transformation*, in *Kyklos*, XV (Fasc. 2, 1962), 855. It represents, however, a modification in the assumption of subsistence incomes. It is not possible to argue that the negative effects of trade can be avoided as soon as the factors of production in the import-competing sector consume only the import-competing product, since if they consume no other products they sell no products and thus they do not constitute a real import-competing sector. The avoidance of underemployment, and the further negative effects due to the complete absence of an import-competing sector, is a different case, which will be discussed further below.

4. The argument that production of vent-for-surplus goods might be taken up represents some modification of the assumption of no reallocation. However, there is a great difference between responding to the necessity for rapid reallocation and the gradual building up of a new activity.

5. Myint, "The 'Classical Theory' of International Trade and the Underdeveloped Countries."

6. See Linder, *An Essay on Trade and Transformation*, pp. 24–28. What was there referred to as "u-countries" corresponds in the present terminology to backward countries. The effects of trade on such countries are taken up anew here, although most briefly, to relate this trade theory to the theory suggested for developing countries. A further reason is to draw policy conclusions, which were not formulated in the original discussion, intended rather as a theoretical exercise.

7. In order to offer some empirical evidence of the existence of such extinction processes in the past, the following three quotations may be made:

a. From J. Strachey, *The End of Empire* (London and New York, 1959 and 1964), p. 52:

> And yet how slowly and with what anguish did the regenerative element in British rule in India begin to emerge out of the purely destructive. The destructive element persisted and predominated far into the nineteenth century. For example, nearly eighty years after the conquest of Bengal a reforming Governor-General, Lord William Cavendish-Bentinck, reported that "the bones of the cotton weavers are bleaching the plains of India." There was, however, this difference between the eighteenth- and the nineteenth-century devastations. The earlier ruin was caused by what was virtually direct plunder thinly disguised as commerce. But what, in the fourth decade of the nineteenth century, was strewing the Indian plains with the bones of her starved cotton weavers was not bad government, corruption or plundering traders. On the contrary, the methods of the British government in India had by then vastly improved. What was having this deadly effect was simply the impact of machine-made Lancashire cotton cloth which undercut the Indian handloom weavers.

The same quotation from Lord Cavendish-Bentinck is also cited by Marx in *Das Kapital*.

b. From C. Woodham-Smith, *The Great Hunger: Ireland 1845–49* (London and New York, 1962 and 1963), p. 16:

> As the years passed, however, no happiness [from political union between England and Ireland in 1801] resulted. The hope of English investment proved a delusion. Free Trade between the two countries enabled England to use Ireland as a market for surplus English goods, Irish industry collapsed, unemployment was widespread, and Dublin, now that an Irish Parliament sat no longer in College Green, became a half-dead city.

    c. From C. P. Fitzgerald, *The Birth of Communist China* (London and Baltimore, Md., 1964), p. 33:

> The Chinese peasant had relied, apart from his fields, on the products of craftsmanship. In winter, at slack seasons, and at all times for the surplus hands, various handicrafts had provided a livelihood. With the import of manufactured goods from the West this rural industry was successively attacked, rendered unproductive, and at last in all the provinces accessible to the ports virtually extinguished.

    Of great interest is also Kindleberger's analysis of the effects on local industry of the spread of modern means of transportation in the industrializing countries in Europe. See his *Economic Growth in France and Britain, 1851–1950* (Cambridge, Mass., 1964), pp. 170 ff. It could also be noted that extinction processes of this kind belong to the group of phenomena that Myrdal has referred to as the "backwash effect." See G. Myrdal, *Economic Theory and Under-Developed Regions* (London, 1957).

    8. Nor would the termination of trade benefit the export sector. It would, in fact, do the opposite, since it would lead to a terms of trade deterioration with effects comparable to those that would arise if foreign demand ceased altogether, i.e., an extinction process would affect the export sector, too.

    9. See, e.g., Wionczek (ed.), *op. cit.*

Chapter 5. Concluding Comments

    1. The possible existence of a fourth category, i.e., of developing countries without an acute foreign-exchange gap, has been noted in the theory section, but disregarded in the policy discussion.

    2. See Haberler, *International Trade and Economic Development*, and "Integration and Growth of the World Economy in Historical Perspective," *American Economic Review*, LIV (March, 1964), 1–22, especially pp. 14 – 19; and Viner, *International Trade and Economic Development*.

    3. Nurkse, *Patterns of Trade and Development*, and Seers, *op. cit.*

    4. Myint, "The 'Classical Theory' of International Trade and the Underdeveloped Countries," and "The Gains from International Trade and the Backward Countries," *Review of Economic Studies*, XXII (1954–55), 129–42.

    5. Prebisch, "Commercial Policy in the Underdeveloped Countries," *American Economic Review*, XLIX (May, 1959), 251–73; H. W. Singer, "The Distribution of Gains between Investing and Borrowing Countries," *American Economic Review*, XL (May, 1950), 473–85; and Myrdal, *op. cit.*

    6. I. G. Patel, *op. cit.;* S. J. Patel, *op. cit.;* Kitamura, "Economic Theory and Regional Economic Integration of Asia"; and Prebisch, *Towards a New Trade Policy for Development*.

Bibliography

Allen, R. L. "Integration in Less Developed Areas," *Kyklos*, XIV (Fasc. 3, 1961), 315–36.

Allen, W. R. "Domestic Investment, the Foreign Trade Balance, and the World Bank," *Kyklos*, XV (Fasc. 2, 1962), 353–73.

Alter, G. M. "The Servicing of Foreign Capital Inflows by Under-Developed Countries," in H. Ellis and H. C. Wallich (eds.). *Economic Development for Latin America*. (Proceedings of a Conference held by the International Economic Association at Rio de Janeiro, August, 1957.) London: Macmillan & Co; New York: St. Martin's Press, 1961.

Avramovic, D. *Debt Servicing Capacity and Postwar Growth in International Indebtedness*. Baltimore, Md.: Johns Hopkins Press, 1958.

Avramovic, D., and R. Gulhati. *Debt Servicing Problems of Low-Income Countries, 1956–1958*. Baltimore, Md.: Johns Hopkins Press, 1960.

Balassa, B. *The Theory of Economic Integration*. Homewood, Ill.: Richard D. Irwin, 1961.

———. "Toward a Theory of Economic Integration," in M. S. Wionczek (ed.). *Latin American Economic Integration* (see below), pp. 21–31.

———. *Trade Prospects for Developing Countries*. (A publication of The Economic Growth Center, Yale University.) Homewood, Ill.: Richard D. Irwin, 1964.

Baldwin, R. E. "Exchange Rate Policy and Economic Development," *Economic Development and Cultural Change*, IX (July, 1961), 598–603.

Bardhan, P. K. "Investment Pattern and the External Balance," *The Economic Weekly* (India), XIV (July, 1962), 1207–10.

Becker, G. S. "Investment in Human Capital: A Theoretical Analysis," *Journal of Political Economy*, LXX, No. 5, Part II (October, 1962), Supplement, 9–49.

Beringer, C. "Real Effects of Foreign Surplus Disposal in Underdeveloped Economies: Comment," *Quarterly Journal of Economics*, LXXVII (May, 1963), 317–23.

Bernstein, E. M. "Some Economic Aspects of Multiple Exchange Rates," *International Monetary Fund Staff Papers*, I (1950–51), 224–37.

Bettelheim, C. *Studies in the Theory of Planning*. Bombay: Asia Publishing House, 1959.

Bhagwati, J. "Indian Balance of Payments Policy and Exchange Auctions," *Oxford Economic Papers*, N. S., XIV (February, 1962), 51–68.

———. "The Theory of Comparative Advantage in the Context of Underdevelopment and Growth," *The Pakistan Development Review*, II (Autumn, 1962), 339–53.

173

Bhambri, R. S. "Customs Unions and Underdeveloped Countries," *Economía Internazionale*, XV (May, 1962), 235–58.

Chenery, H. B. "Comparative Advantage and Development Policy," *American Economic Review*, LI (March, 1961), 18–51.

————, and M. Bruno. "Development Alternatives in an Open Economy: The Case of Israel," *Economic Journal*, LXXII (March, 1962), 79–103.

Dell, S. *Trade Blocs and Common Markets*. London: Constable & Co.; New York: Alfred A. Knopf, 1963.

Dorfman, R., P. A. Samuelson, and R. M. Solow. *Linear Programming and Economic Analysis*. New York: McGraw-Hill, 1958.

Eckaus, R. S. "Factor Proportions in Underdeveloped Areas," *American Economic Review*, XLV (September, 1955), 539–65.

Falcon, W. P. "Real Effects of Foreign Surplus Disposal in Underdeveloped Economies: Further Comment," *Quarterly Journal of Economics*, LXXII (May, 1963), 323–26.

Federal Reserve Bank of New York. "The Emerging Common Markets in Latin America," *Monthly Review*, XLII (September, 1960), 154–60.

Finch, D. "Investment Service of Underdeveloped Countries," *International Monetary Fund Staff Papers*, II (September, 1951), 60–85.

Fitzgerald, C. P. *The Birth of Communist China*. London and Baltimore, Md.: Penguin Books, 1964.

Fleming, M. "On Making the Best of Balance of Payments Restrictions on Imports," *Economic Journal*, LXI (March, 1951), 48–71.

Friedman, M. "The Case for Flexible Exchange Rates," *Essays in Positive Economics*. Chicago: University of Chicago Press, 1953. Pp. 157–203.

Gal-Edd, I. *The General Agreement on Tariffs and Trade and the Developing Nations*. Israel: Government Printing Press, May, 1961.

General Agreement on Tariffs and Trade. *Basic Instruments and Selected Documents. Eleventh Supplement*. (Sales No.: GATT/1963–1.) Geneva, March, 1963.

————. *International Trade 1956*. (Sales No.: GATT/1957-2.) Geneva, June, 1957.

————. *International Trade 1959*. (Sales No.: GATT/1960-3.) Geneva, 1960.

————. *International Trade 1961*. (Sales No.: GATT/1962-5.) Geneva, September, 1962.

————. *Trends in International Trade*. A Report by a Panel of Experts. (G. Haberler, J. E. Meade, R. de Oliveira Campos, J. Tinbergen.) (Sales No.: GATT/1958-3.) Geneva, October, 1958.

Golay, F. H. *The Philippines: Public Policy and National Economic Development*. Ithaca, N.Y.: Cornell University Press, 1961.

Government of India, Ministry of Commerce and Industry. *Report of the Import and Export Policy Committee*. New Delhi: Government of India Press, 1962.

————. Planning Commission. *Third Five Year Plan*, New Delhi: Government of India Press, 1961.

Haberler, G. "Integration and Growth of the World Economy in Historical Perspective," *American Economic Review*, LIV (March, 1964), 1–22.

————. *International Trade and Economic Development*. (National

Bank of Egypt, Fiftieth Anniversary Commemoration Lectures.) Cairo: National Bank of Egypt Printing Press, 1959.

————. "Some Problems in the Pure Theory of International Trade," *Economic Journal*, LX (June, 1950), 223—40.

Hagen, E. E. "An Economic Justification of Protectionism," *Quarterly Journal of Economics*, LXII (November, 1958), 496—514.

Harberger, A. C. "Using Resources at Hand More Effectively," *American Economic Review*, XLIX (May, 1959), 134—46.

Harrod, R. "Economic Development and Asian Regional Cooperation," *The Pakistan Development Review*, II (Spring, 1962), 1—22.

Hart, A. G., and P. B. Kenen. *Money, Debt, and Economic Activity.* 3d ed.; Englewood Cliffs, N. J.: Prentice-Hall, 1961.

Hemming, M. F. W., and W. M. Corden. "Import Restriction as an Instrument of Balance-of-Payments Policy," *Economic Journal*, LXVIII (September, 1958), 483—510.

Higgins, B. *Economic Development.* New York: W. W. Norton, 1959.

Hirschman, A. O. (ed.). *Latin American Issues: Essays and Comments.* New York: Twentieth Century Fund, 1961.

————. *The Strategy of Economic Development* (Yale Studies in Economics, No. 10.) New Haven, Conn.: Yale University Press, 1958.

International Monetary Fund. *Yearbook on Exchange Restrictions.* Washington, D. C., various years.

Johnson, H. G. *International Trade and Economic Growth.* Cambridge, Mass.: Harvard University Press, 1958.

————. "Optimum Tariffs and Retaliation," *Review of Economic Studies*, XXI (1953—54), 142—53.

Kafka, A. "The Brazilian Exchange Auction System," *Review of Economics and Statistics*, XXXVIII (August, 1956), 308—22.

Kemp, M. C. "The Mill-Bastable Infant-Industry Dogma," *Journal of Political Economy*, LXVIII (February, 1960), 65—67.

Kenen, P. B. "Development, Mobility and the Case for Tariffs: A Dissenting Note," *Kyklos*, XVI (Fasc. 2, 1963), 321—24.

————. Review of S. B. Linder, *An Essay on Trade and Transformation*, *Kyklos*, XVI (Fasc. 4, 1962), 854—56.

Khatkhate, D. R. "Some Notes on the Real Effects of Foreign Surplus Disposal in Underdeveloped Countries' Economies," *Quarterly Journal of Economics*, LXXVI (May, 1962), 186—96.

Kindleberger, C. P. *Economic Development.* New York: McGraw-Hill, 1958.

————. *Economic Growth in France and Britain, 1851—1950.* Cambridge, Mass.: Harvard University Press, 1964.

————. *International Economics.* 3d ed.; Homewood, Ill.: Richard D. Irwin, 1963.

Kitamura, H. "Economic Theory and the Economic Integration of Underdeveloped Regions," in M. S. Wionczek (ed.). *Latin American Economic Integration* (see below), pp. 42—63.

————. "Economic Theory and Regional Economic Integration of Asia," *The Pakistan Development Review*, II (Winter, 1962), 485—504.

Lakdawala, D. T. "Aspects of Trade Policy in India," *Indian Economic Journal*, XII (October-December, 1964), 89—110.

————. "Trade Cooperation Within the ECAFE Region," *The Pakistan Development Review*, II (Winter, 1962), 505—42.

League of Nations (Haberler, G.). *Quantitative Trade Controls: Their Causes and Nature.* (League of Nations Publications, Economic and Financial 1943, No. II.A.5.) Geneva, 1943.

Lewis, W. A. "Economic Development and World Trade." (Submitted to the International Congress on Economic Development organized by the International Economic Association.) Vienna, 1962. Mimeo.

Linder, S. B. "Customs Unions and Economic Development," in W. S. Wionczek (ed.). *Latin American Economic Integration* (see below), pp. 32–41.

———. *An Essay on Trade and Transformation.* Göteborg and Uppsala and New York: Almqvist & Wiksells and John Wiley, 1961.

———. *The Significance of GATT for Under-Developed Countries.* (U. N. Doc. E/CONF. 46/P/6.) Geneva, 1964. Mimeo.

Lipsey, R. O. "The Theory of Customs Unions: A General Survey," *Economic Journal,* LXX (September, 1960), 496–513.

Little, I. M. D. Review of W. B. Reddaway's, *The Development of the Indian Economy,* in *Economic Journal,* LXXII (September, 1962), 722–23.

Machlup, F. "Three Concepts of the Balance of Payments and the So-Called Dollar Shortage," *Economic Journal,* LX (March, 1950), 46–68.

McKinnon, R. I. "Foreign Exchange Constraints in Economic Development and Efficient Aid Allocation," *Economic Journal,* LXXIV (June, 1964), 388–409.

Manne, A. S. "Key Sectors of the Mexican Economy, 1960–1970," in A. S. Manne and H. M. Markowitz (eds.). *Studies in Process Analysis.* New York: John Wiley, 1963.

Marshall, J. "Exchange Controls and Economic Development," in H. Ellis and H. C. Wallich (eds.). *Economic Development for Latin America.*

Massell, B. F. "East African Economic Union: An Evaluation and Some Implications for Policy." (Rand Corporation Memorandum RM-3880-RC.) Santa Monica, Calif., December, 1963. Mimeo.

———. "Export Concentration and Fluctuations in Export Earnings: A Cross-Section Analysis," *American Economic Review,"* LIV (March, 1964), 47–63.

Meade, J. E. *The Theory of Customs Unions.* Amsterdam: North Holland Publishing Co., 1955.

———. *The Theory of International Economic Policy.* Vol. I: *The Balance of Payments.* London and New York: Oxford University Press, 1951.

Mikesell, R. F. "The Capacity to Service Foreign Investment," in R. F. Mikesell (ed.). *U. S. Private and Government Investment Abroad.* Eugene, Ore.: University of Oregon Books, 1962. Chap. xiv.

———. "The Movement Toward Regional Trading Groups in Latin America," in A. O. Hirschmann (ed.). *Latin American Issues.* Pp. 125–51.

———. *Public Foreign Capital for Private Enterprise in Developing Countries.* (Princeton Essays in International Finance, No. 52.) Princeton, N.J.: Princeton University Press, 1966.

———. "The Theory of Common Markets as Applied to Regional Arrangements Among Developing Countries," in R. Harrod and D. C. Hague (eds.). *International Trade Theory in a Developing World.*

(Proceedings of a Conference held by the International Economic Association.) London: Macmillan; New York: St. Martin's Press, 1963.
————. (ed.). *U. S. Private and Government Investment Abroad.* Eugene, Ore.: University of Oregon Books, 1962.
Millikan, M. M., and W. W. Rostow. *A Proposal: Key to an Effective Foreign Policy.* New York: Harper & Brothers, 1957.
Mundell, R. A. "The International Disequilibrium System," *Kyklos,* XIV (Fasc. 2, 1961), 153–72.
Myint, H. "The Classical Theory of International Trade and the Underdeveloped Countries," *Economic Journal,* LXVII (June, 1958), 317–37.
————. "The Gains from International Trade and the Backward Countries," *Review of Economic Studies,* XXII (1954–55), 129–42.
————. "Infant Industry Arguments for Assistance to Industries in the Setting of Dynamic Trade Theory," in R. Harrod and D. C. Hague (eds.). *International Trade Theory in a Developing World.*
Myrdal, G. *Economic Theory and Under-Developed Regions.* London: Gerald Duckworth, 1957.
National Industrial Conference Board. "Obstacles to Trade Between Developed and Developing Nations," *The Conference Board Record,* I, No. 11 (November, 1964), 23–46.
Nurkse, R. "Domestic and International Equilibrium," in S. E. Harris (ed.). *The New Economics: Keynes' Influence on Theory and Public Policy.* New York: Alfred A. Knopf, 1947. Pp. 264–92.
————. *Patterns of Trade and Development.* (Wiksells Lectures, 1959.) Stockholm: Almqvist & Wiksells, 1959.
Patel, I. G. "Trade and Payments Policy for a Developing Economy," in R. Harrod and D. C. Hague (eds.). *International Trade Theory in a Developing World.*
Patel, S. J. "Export Prospects and Economic Growth: India," *Economic Journal,* LXIX (September, 1959), 490–506.
Prebisch, R. "Commercial Policy in the Underdeveloped Countries," *American Economic Review,* XLIX (May, 1959), 251–73.
Pryor, F. L. *The Communist Foreign Trade System.* London: George Allen & Unwin; Cambridge, Mass.: The M.I.T. Press, 1963.
Royer, J. *In Defence of GATT.* (Conference on New Directions for World Trade, September 16–24, 1963.) London: Royal Institute of International Affairs, 1963.
Schlesinger, E. R. *Multiple Exchange Rates and Economic Development.* (Princeton Studies in International Finance, Vol. II.) Princeton, N.J.: Princeton University Press, 1952.
Schultz, T. W. "Value of U. S. Farm Surplus to Underdeveloped Countries," *Journal of Farm Economics,* XLII (December, 1960), 1019–30.
Seers, D. "A Model of Comparative Rates of Growth in the World Economy," *Economic Journal,* LXXII (March, 1962), 45–78.
Singer, H. W. "The Distribution of Gains between Investing and Borrowing Countries," *American Economic Review,* XL (May, 1950), 473–85.
Strachey, J. *The End of Empire.* London: Victor Gollancz, 1959. Paperback ed.; New York: Frederick A. Praeger, 1964.
Tinbergen, J. *The Design of Development.* (The Economic Development

Institute, International Bank for Reconstruction and Development.)
Baltimore, Md.: Johns Hopkins Press, 1958.
United Nations. "Co-ordination of Development Plans in Africa," *Economic Bulletin for Africa*, IV, No. 1, Part B (January, 1964), 1–69.
————. *Monthly Bulletin of Statistics*, Special Table E, XV (March, 1961), xviii–xxxi; Special Table B, XV (April, 1961), xxiii–xx; Special Table B, XVIII (January, 1964), xii–xv; Special Table C, XVIII (March, 1964), xiv–xxvii; Special Table B, XVIII (April, 1964), xviii–xx; Special Table C, XX (March, 1966), xii.
————. *Statistical Yearbook, 1964.* (U. N. Sales No.: 65.XVII.1.) New York, 1965.
————. (Prebisch, R.) *Towards a New Trade Policy for Development.* (Report by the Secretary-General of the United Nations Conference on Trade and Development.) New York, 1964.
————. *World Economic Survey, 1962.* Part I: *The Developing Countries in World Trade.* (U.N. Sales No.: 63.II.C.1.) New York, 1963.
————. *World Economic Survey, 1963.* Part I: *Trade and Development: Trends, Needs and Policies.* (U.N. Sales No.: 64.II.C.1.) New York, 1964.
United Nations Conference on Trade and Development. "The Developing Countries in GATT." (U. N. Doc. E/CONF. 46/36.) Geneva: United Nations, March, 1964. Mimeo.
————. "Economic Growth and External Debt—An Analytical Framework." (A paper prepared by the Staff of the International Bank for Reconstruction and Development.) (U.N. Doc. E/CONF. 46/84.) Geneva, March, 1964. Mimeo.
————. "Economic Growth and External Debt—A Statistical Presentation." (A paper prepared by the Staff of the International Bank for Reconstruction and Development.) (U.N. Doc. E/CONF. 46/40.) Geneva, March, 1964. Mimeo.
————. "The Role of GATT in Relation to Trade and Development." (A paper prepared by the GATT Secretariat.) (U.N. Doc. E/CONF. 46/38.) Geneva, March, 1964. Mimeo.
United Nations Economic Commission for Africa. "Report of the ECA Industrial Co-ordination Mission to Algeria, Libya, Morocco, and Tunisia." (U.N. Doc. E/CN. 14/248.) Addis Ababa, 1964. Mimeo.
————. "Report of the ECA Industrial Co-ordination Mission to East and Central Africa." (U.N. Doc. E/CN. 14/247.) Addis Ababa, 1964. Mimeo.
————. Report of the West African Industrial Co-ordination Mission." (U.N. Doc. E/CN. 14/246.) Addis Ababa, 1964. Mimeo.
United Nations Economic Commission for Latin America. "General Situation and Future Outlook of the Central American Integration Program." (U.N. Doc. E/CN. 12/666.) Mar del Plata, May, 1963. Mimeo.
————. The Latin American Common Market. (U.N. Sales No.: 59.II. G.4.) New York, United Nations, 1959.
————. (Prebisch, R.) *Towards a Dynamic Development Policy for Latin America.* (U.N. Sales No.: 64.II.G.4.) New York, 1964.
Urquidi, V. L. "The Common Market as a Tool of Latin America's Economic Development: A Comment," in A. O. Hirschman (ed.). *Latin American Issues.* Pp. 151–60.

————. *Free Trade and Economic Integration in Latin America.* Translated by M. M. Urquidi. Berkeley and Los Angeles, Calif.: University of California Press, 1962.

Veblen, T. *The Theory of Business Enterprise.* New York: Charles Scribner's Sons, 1904.

Vernon, R. "A Trade Policy for the 1960's," *Foreign Affairs,* XXXIX (April, 1961), 458–70.

Viner, J. *The Customs Union Issue.* New York: Carnegie Endowment for International Peace, 1950.

————. *International Trade and Economic Development.* Oxford: Clarendon Press, 1953.

Waterston, A. "Development Planning: Lessons of Experience." To be published by Economic Development Institute, International Bank of Reconstruction and Development.

Wionczek, M. S. (ed.). *Latin American Economic Integration: Experiences and Prospects.* New York: Frederick A. Praeger, 1966. See particularly his Introduction.

————. "The Montevideo Treaty and Latin American Economic Integration," *Banca Nazionale del Lavoro Quarterly Review,* LVII (June, 1961), 197–240.

Woodham-Smith, C. *The Great Hunger: Ireland 1845–49.* London: Hamish Hamilton, 1962; New York: Harper & Row, 1963.

Woods, G. C. Address at the Annual Meeting of the International Bank for Reconstruction and Development, Fall, 1963. Reprinted in *International Financial News Survey,* XV (October 4, 1963), 338–42.